10,000 Babies:
My life in the delivery room

10,000 Babies:
My life in the delivery room

SILVIO ALADJEM MD

authorHOUSE®

AuthorHouse™
1663 Liberty Drive
Bloomington, IN 47403
www.authorhouse.com
Phone: 1-800-839-8640

Published by AuthorHouse   02/20/2013

ISBN: 978-1-4817-1459-4 (sc)
ISBN: 978-1-4817-1460-0 (hc)

Library of Congress Control Number: 2013903173

About the cover:
Mother and child
Bronze by Trudy Mueller
Contemporary American
From a private collection
Reproduced by permission

This book is printed on acid-free paper.

DEDICATION

This book is dedicated, with all my love, to Judith, my wife, friend, and soul mate. Without her support, encouragement and unshakable belief that I can do it, this book would have never seen the light of day.

*A tribute to all the mothers I had the privilege
to take care of.*

ABOUT THE AUTHOR

Silvio Aladjem MD, FACOG, FRSM, is Professor Emeritus in Obstetrics and Gynecology at the College of Human Medicine, Michigan State University in Lansing, MI. and Clinical Professor of Obstetrics and Gynecology at Wayne State University in Detroit, MI. He is Board Certified in both Obstetrics and Gynecology and the sub-specialty of Maternal Fetal Medicine.

He is a member of many professional and scientific organizations, including the American College of Obstetricians and Gynecologists (ACOG), American Medical Association (AMA), Michigan State Medical Society (MSMS), Society of Maternal Fetal Medicine (SMFM) and others including the Royal Society of Medicine in the United Kingdom.

He is the author of several textbooks of Obstetrics and Perinatal Medicine. In addition, he has published extensively in professional scientific journals in the US, UK, Europe and South America. His textbooks have been translated and published in Europe and South America.

TABLE OF CONTENTS

ABOUT THE AUTHOR   vii

INTRODUCTION   xi

SECTION 1: AT THE START OF THE JOURNEY   1

How my journey began   3
Modern miracles   10
"I can't be pregnant—I'm on the pill!"   16
I don't want to know   21
Does genetic screening have all the answers?   24
I am sick every morning   29
What are we going to do?   34
When can she get pregnant again?   38
What do you mean it's more than one?   45
A little blood is scary   62

SECTION 2: ALONG THE WAY   69

Myths and facts of pregnancy   71
An unusual headache   76
Will my baby be born early?   80
Just give me a hug   94
When the heart fails   99
Hospital by helicopter   110
Mozart or rock and roll?   115

SECTION 3: THE MOMENT OF TRUTH   129

A matter of experience   131
I want him there!   137
Kids having kids   141
Where's the baby?   148
My twin brother is weeks younger than me   154
Different cultures, different labors   163
Timing is everything   176
Unforgettable moments   183

SECTION 4: IN A CLASS OF THEIR OWN   193

A mother's secret   195
A labor of love   200
Against the odds   203
It's not my baby!   210
Who is the father?   219
What's for dinner?   227
Special staff for a special task   231

AUTHOR'S NOTE   235

ACKNOWLEDGEMENTS   239

INTRODUCTION

Throughout my forty years of obstetrical practice, the first cry of a newborn has always been an exceptional thrill for me. This first cry is the quintessence of life itself; there is nothing quite like it. The birth of a child, however, is but the end of nine long months, during which two unrelated individuals—the mother to be and her obstetrician—establish a temporary and unusual bond with a common purpose in mind.

The future mother wants a healthy baby, and the obstetrician guides and cares for her so that this goal should become a reality. This is a most unusual commonality of purpose, not only in scope but also in time, unlike any other in the practice of medicine. It is not surprising, therefore, that a variety of events, over and beyond medical care, will occur. When I look back on my four decades of being part of the lives of others for the sole purpose of bringing a new life into this world, I cannot but feel privileged and humbled. Over the years, I have witnessed events of all kinds. Some were funny, and some were plain silly. Others were emotionally exhausting, and several were tragic. But all of them, without exception, were profoundly human—events from which we learn about ourselves, about others, about life, love, joy, sorrow, and about who we are.

The labor and delivery area is a place like no other in a hospital. It can be as quiet as the city library, but then, from one moment to the next, can suddenly become chaotic. That is why I particularly like one definition of obstetrics which states:

"Obstetrics is long hours of boredom superseded with moments of terror." Whoever came up with this definition knew labor and delivery! But labor and delivery is also the final step in having a baby. It is where the anxious family awaits the new arrival; where, sometimes, the mother- and father-to-be appear to have never seen each other before; where relations are strengthened or begin to disintegrate; where "it's a boy" or "it's a girl" is called for the first time; or where a lonely woman is left sobbing when no one is there to hug her.

Over its nine-month duration, pregnancy can be challenging, not only for the mother-to-be but for her obstetrician. Things happen—like the time a patient of mine was having a hard time with early pregnancy nausea and vomiting. Nothing seemed to help, and at one of her visits, this young lady stunned me with the question: "You don't think I could vomit the baby, do you?" Given the hard time she was having, I understood her desperation, and I reassured her that this would not happen. A few weeks later, when calm returned, she asked me to please not tell anyone about her silly question. I replied: "What question?"

Another time, an angry father walked out of the delivery room after his wife had just given birth to a baby girl—the third one in the family. He had fully expected a boy this time. I was appalled. I followed him and reminded him that he was the one responsible for the birth of a girl, since the sperm, and not the egg, determines the sex of a baby. I told him a few other things, too, and he eventually returned to the delivery room to be at his wife's side.

The purpose of this book is to share with you such stories. You may find that some sound familiar. Others will not. These are real human stories surrounding the most important event of our lives: the birthing of our children—as complex a phenomenon as it can be simple. As joyous as it can be painful. It can be normal or abnormal. It can lift our spirits, or it can challenge the core of our fortitude. As a Maternal Fetal Medicine Specialist, the last in the chain of medical consultations for complicated pregnancies, I was witness to the anxieties that parents have to go through when confronted with uncertainty about the fate of their expected child. Believe me, it leaves its mark. It is only compensated by the rewards of the joy when a healthy child is born and the mother is well.

In order to structure the book, I have grouped together stories with a common theme. Stories relating to the beginning of pregnancy have little common ground with those relating to labor and delivery. Furthermore, not all of these stories are simple or funny; some, unfortunately, deal with grief and sorrow, or with deep emotions and profound questions, religious or otherwise. By perusing the contents of the book, you can choose which you would prefer to read at any given time, without losing continuity. When a name is attached to a story, understand that it is not the individual's real name. In the interests of confidentiality, I have done my best to obscure any personal or identifying information. Any similarity to a given individual is merely coincidental.

Each story is an indelible memory in my mind. I cherish them. These moments are part of my life, too, and for them, I am grateful.

Last but not least, over the years. I delivered some 10,000 babies, hence the title of the book.

* * *

SECTION 1:

AT THE START OF THE JOURNEY

How my journey began

Me, an obstetrician? That was never going to happen. In medical
school, I did the clerkship and passed with flying colors, but I
was not impressed by the specialty. Long hours, sleepless nights,
women in pain for whom we did little. Midwives performed the
deliveries and only called the doctor "if needed." Besides, OB was
messy. There was blood all over the bed, the floor, on the midwife
or the doctor. And then, once the baby was delivered, chances were
the first thing the little one would do, after crying, was pee on the
midwife or doctor! No, obstetrics was definitely not for me!

I was going to be a cardiologist. I was fascinated by the physiology
of the heart, an organ like no other in the body. I was so impressed
by how perfectly it worked that I decided to do a special rotation
during the last year of medical school, simply to learn more about
cardiology.

At that point in time, coronary bypasses, stents, pacemakers,
echocardiograms and other marvels of technology were still to be
invented or not yet in practice. The drugs available today to treat heart
disease had not yet been discovered. If you were born with a serious
heart defect, you most likely did not survive. Children who suffered
rheumatic heart disease as a result of a strep throat were common.

The only technology cardiologists had was the stethoscope and an
EKG machine. A cardiologist would listen to a patient's heart, look
at the EKG tracings, and make his diagnosis. Yes, this was the field
for me. I could see myself making a sophisticated diagnosis and
then discussing, at length, with my colleagues how the physiology
of the heart had changed. I was looking forward to my advanced
clerkship in cardiology.

Two weeks later, on a Monday morning, I started my special rotation
on the cardiology wards. The residents were delighted. I was the
only medical student in the ward for the next six weeks, which
meant I got to do all the "scut" work: admit the patient, undertake
a general examination, follow the patient daily, and be available to

the residents for whatever they needed. I did not mind. I was finally doing what I thought I wanted to do for the rest of my life.

At 10 am sharp, the professor of cardiology arrived on the ward to make his rounds. The residents were ready to present the history, current diagnosis, and treatment of each patient to him. However, when rounds finished that day, something was bothering me. I could not figure out what.

After one week, the feeling only grew and grew. I felt uneasy. My original enthusiasm had waned, yet I still could not understand why. Following an incident in the ER one night, it became apparent to me what this feeling was all about.

I saw a patient in the ER and admitted him to the hospital. He was fifty-five years old and known to the cardiology service. He had been admitted several times over the past few years because he had an aortic insufficiency; his aortic valve was unable to close properly, which allowed blood to flow backwards into the left ventricle of his heart. Over time, because the heart was unable to pump all of the extra blood, it became enlarged, and he developed a cardiac insufficiency. At that point in time, the only treatment available was digoxin, which was supposed to strengthen the heart's contraction. However, he was beyond that point, and there was no effective treatment for his rampant aortic insufficiency or his severe cardiac failure. Today, it is a routine procedure to replace a faulty aortic valve, and is performed long before the heart is failing.

None of us had any hope for him. We did not think he would be able to pull out of it this time. All we could do was keep him comfortable. Oxygen helped, but progressively, he found breathing increasingly difficult. His family was with him, and we tried to comfort them as much as we could. He had died early that morning.

It was not the first time I had seen someone die in the hospital. The death of this man, however, was somehow different. Over several years of aortic insufficiency, the disease had worsened year after year and there was nothing, at that time, that medicine could do to help him.

A week later, we had cardiology Grand Rounds in the hospital amphitheater. Grand Rounds are scientific gatherings at which a patient's case is presented and a professor discusses the disease, treatment and prognosis. Cardiologists, other doctors from different specialties, residents and medical students, were all in attendance. Two patients the professor of cardiology had never seen before were brought into the amphitheater and presented to him for his evaluation. After examining the patients and reviewing the supporting information (laboratory, X-rays, EKGs) he made his diagnosis, explained how he reached it, and outlined his treatment plan to the audience. A lecture and lengthy discussion followed. These sessions were an extraordinary learning experience.

After Grand Rounds, I finally realized what was bothering me and why my enthusiasm for cardiology had vanished. With the medicines and technology available at that time, nothing much could be done for patients with cardiac disease. Ultimately, once the heart began to fail, for whatever reason, there was little we could do about it. A cardiologist, no matter how good, could not alter the inevitable course of the disease. Maybe he could slow it down a little, but there was no conclusive cure for anything.

The inability to heal or reverse the disease and the inability to positively intervene, were facts that I could not live with. The thought that all of my patients would die because I could not help them, was unbearable. I had the same feeling when I saw patients die from incurable cancers. I realized at that moment that cardiology was not for me.

I sometimes think back to the day I told the professor and head of cardiology that I would not be pursuing a residency in cardiology. When he asked why, I remembered what my father used to say to me: "You will never go wrong with the truth." I took a deep breath and started to explain my feelings.
"I love everything about cardiology, except for the practice of cardiology. We never cure anyone, and I find that depressing and frustrating."

5

To my amazement, he understood and agreed. "Cardiology", he told me, "is still in its infancy. We do the best with what we have. Someday, we will have the drugs and techniques to cure what we cannot now."

I often think of him, and what he would say about the marvelous medicines and surgeries that can save, prolong, and improve a cardiac patient's life today. Nowadays, if my patient with aortic insufficiency had come to the ER, he would have had a surgically implanted new aortic valve long before his heart failed. He would have lived.

I decided I needed a short vacation to try to regain perspective about my future in medicine. One day, I met with my friend Tom, a medical student, for lunch. We talked about our shared experiences in medical school and, of course, Tom wanted to know what my plans were after graduation. He was shocked to learn that I didn't know.
"Why don't you take another look at OB?" he asked.
"Obstetrics! Why?"
"It's really exciting," Tom said. "There is nothing like the birth of a baby, and you deal with healthy young patients." Tom had taken his clerkship in Professor Dr. Alvarez's service. "He is doing very exciting new work in uterine physiology with Dr. Caldeyro in a new department called Obstetrical Physiology," Tom continued. "They are finally beginning to learn what goes on when the uterus is contracting during labor. Doctors are coming from all over the world to learn and work there."

Reluctantly, I agreed to stop by and see this new department and figure out what all the excitement was about. First, of course, I needed the approval of Professors Alvarez and Caldeyro.

I was granted permission to be in the research lab for two weeks. Little did I know the profound and life-changing effect the next two weeks would have on me.

That Monday morning, I arrived at the Uterine Physiology Research Lab in the Hospital de Clinicas—the University's main hospital. A young woman in early labor was on the bed. Dr. Alvarez, I was told, was preparing to monitor her labor by using a thin catheter placed inside the uterus.

Now, you must understand that at that point in time no one had any concept of what the physiology of the uterus was during labor. We knew little, if anything, about the physiology of the fetus during its intrauterine life. The uterus was considered an inviolable place, and the mere idea of placing a needle, blindly, inside a pregnant uterus was considered an anathema. Yet, that was exactly what I was about to witness.

Dr. Alvarez first cleaned the patient's abdomen with antiseptic. Then he covered her abdomen with sterile surgical towels and took out, from a sterilized metal box, a small needle and syringe. From a vial, he drew some local anesthetic and proceeded to inject it into the abdominal skin, reassuring the patient that in a minute she would feel no more pain than, at most, a mosquito bite. Once the local anesthetic had taken effect, he removed a long, large needle from the box, and with a firm hand, pushed it through the abdominal wall into the uterus. The patient did not move. Clear amniotic fluid started flowing. Without hesitation, he threaded a fine catheter through the needle inside the uterus. Fluid began flowing through the catheter. He then pulled the needle out of the abdomen and through the open end of the catheter. Dr. Alvarez handed the catheter to an assistant, who proceeded to connect it to the recording machine. Instantly, a recording needle started moving slowly up and down on the recording paper. Dr. Caldeyro took a look at the paper and said, "We are OK."

Dr. Alvarez then removed the sterile towels from the patient's abdomen and, using a sterile tape, secured the fine catheter to woman's abdomen. "I did not hurt you, did I?" he asked the patient. "No" she replied.
"Good. If you have any questions, just ask." The whole procedure had taken at most one to two minutes. The pregnant uterus, we were told, was inviolable. No more!

My throat was dry and my heart was pounding. I had seen many other procedures performed for a variety of reasons, but none had ever had that effect on me. I was frozen in time. Over my obstetrical clerkship, it was made clear to me that obstetrics was the only branch of medicine where we take care of two patients simultaneously but can talk to and examine only one. The inability to obtain direct information from the second patient is a big handicap.

Throughout her labor, all of the woman's contractions were recorded, and after some six hours, she delivered a healthy baby girl.

The first week I was there just flew by. I started reading as much as I could about the methodologies used in the research lab, and about the preliminary results available. Slowly but surely, I felt I could begin to understand and discuss what the others were talking about. Sometimes during one's life, a single event can leave a profound and lasting impression that culminates in a life-changing moment; that was what was happening to me.

During my second week, a patient who was only about five feet tall was in labor with her first baby. Her uterus was large, and I estimated her baby to weigh more than nine pounds. Could she deliver vaginally? Dr. Alvarez examined her and found that her pelvis was small and that the baby was large. "We will let you labor for a while and see what happens," he said. "But," he added, "you will most likely need a cesarean section."

We began to monitor the pressure inside her uterus. I was listening to the baby's heart and recording the rate. By palpating the abdominal wall during contraction, I could feel the uterus contract. By watching the pressure recording, I could see and feel, minute by minute, what was happening. This experience gave me a new perspective on what labor is really all about. It soon became obvious that the uterine pressure recordings were decreasing in intensity and that labor was slowing down. What was happening? Why this pattern in the recordings? Why was her labor slowing? A natural safety mechanism was beginning to take over. Contractions slowed because the baby was too large for its head to descend into

8

the pelvis for vaginal delivery. If the uterus continued to contract at the same rate and force, it could rupture the uterus, damaging the baby and potentially threatening the life of the mother.

Dr. Alvarez decided the time had come for a cesarean section. I was asked to be a second assistant during the section and, as such, I witnessed the birth of a healthy ten-pound baby boy.

The following day, I was asked to present the case to the entire staff of the research lab during the morning conference. During the discussion about this patient, I began to realize I was hooked. OB was where my heart was. Yes, my future was going to be taking care of pregnant patients and using all of my training and future know-how to deliver healthy infants.

The work of Drs. Alvarez and Caldeyro was innovative and ground-breaking in obstetrics. They described and defined uterine physiology throughout pregnancy, as well as in normal and abnormal labor. Every textbook of obstetrics, now and for the foreseeable future, no matter where published, reproduces those original labor graphs.

* * *

Modern miracles

Before the eighteenth century, a pregnant woman was attended to at home by a midwife, and men were excluded from the bedroom in which labor and delivery occurred. By the mid-eighteenth century, physicians—who were all men—started paying attention to the care of pregnant women, much to the dismay of midwives and the public at large. As physicians became involved in parturition, lying-in hospitals made their appearance. These hospitals were initially designed with the pregnant woman in mind. Usually, poor women came to have their babies at these hospitals, and since they were charity hospitals, the care was free. Generally speaking, however, most labor and deliveries continued to occur at home, with midwives in charge.

During the nineteenth century, little, if any, progress was made. In England, for example, obstetrics was not taught in medical school and it was thought that such care should be provided by midwives exclusively. While lying-in hospitals continued to exist, physician practices did not include pregnant women and prenatal care was unknown. With time, however, male midwives appeared and obstetrics became part of the training of a physician. Few physicians, however, would refer to themselves as obstetricians. Midwives with formal training had to be certified, which decreased the number of "lay midwives," who had no medical education.

Historically, maternal mortality was high, due primarily to "childbirth fever," also known as "puerperal fever." Dr. Semmelweis, a Hungarian physician, showed in the mid-nineteenth century how doctors could reduce childbirth fever by simply washing their hands. Physicians did not accept his views, and they continued to attend a woman in labor after just having performed an autopsy! It was not until the beginning of the twentieth century that the importance of asepsis—a technique to keep everything a doctor works with germ-free, was finally accepted and implemented during childbirth.

Delivery, however, continued to occur primarily at home, and it still does in many parts of the world. In the US and Western Europe, labor and delivery moved slowly from the home to the hospitals at the beginning of the twentieth century. The concept of prenatal care appeared for the first time in Boston in around 1900, where clinics were established for the care of pregnant women. The focus of such clinics was the early detection of pregnancy complications such as preeclampsia, which can kill a baby and its mother if not taken care of properly.

During the first fifty years of the twentieth century, no major changes in the practice of obstetrics occurred. The focus was on understanding the causes of maternal mortality. As late as 1935, for example, 12,544 women died annually in the United States as a result of pregnancy. Efforts were, therefore, mostly directed towards reducing such mortality by applying knowledge gained from autopsies of pregnant women who died during labor and delivery.

Scientific understanding of the physiology of pregnancy, labor, and delivery, was limited. The fetus was unreachable, and what medical professionals knew about the unborn baby was minimal or wrong. The impact of the death of a baby before birth was usually minimized, and obstetricians used to tell mothers to just try again. There was little understanding of how maternal medical or surgical problems unrelated to pregnancy affected the pregnancy or the fetus.

In both the United States and Western Europe, the first half of the twentieth century was dedicated to understanding the physiology and pathology of pregnancy and how such an understanding should be applied to improve the care of pregnant women. Animal research, both in the US and Europe, focused on understanding fetal physiology so that human fetal physiology could be better understood. Slowly, but surely, obstetrics enriched its scientific knowledge, which, together with the technological advances starting in the fifties and sixties, entirely changed the practice of obstetrics.

By 1950, most deliveries were occurring in a hospital environment and were performed by certified obstetricians. Hospitals had to adjust and create new units known as obstetrical units. It was not until the sixties that special units, known as neonatal units, became equipped to render care to premature babies and newborns with special care needs, which in addition to nurseries, became available in most major US hospitals.

Initially, a labor and delivery area was just a big room with beds separated by curtains. That was the extent of privacy for women in labor. After delivery, the infant was cleaned, washed, dressed and moved to a nursery, where a pediatrician would see the infant within twenty-four hours. Newborns were considered "small children" and the pediatrician was their doctor. If the infant had a problem, or was premature, he or she was placed in an "incubator," which kept the baby warm and supplied oxygen; not much else could be done. The medical technology was simply not there yet. It was also thought that the higher the oxygen concentration available to the baby in the incubator, the better; unfortunately, many of those premature infants were blinded by the excessive oxygen.

Once delivered, the mother was taken to either a room or a ward, depending on the hospital and on how much money the patient could afford to pay. After delivery, a mother used to stay in the hospital for up to a week! Parents were not allowed to enter the nursery for fear that the infants may get an infection. They could see their babies through a glass window only. Formula feeding became the norm, and breastfeeding went out of style.

With this background and history, it took a long time for hospitals to adapt to the avalanche of knowledge that was becoming available in the late fifties and early sixties. Obstetrical and pediatric units, including labor and delivery areas, were beginning to see major changes and restructuring. The "incubator" was being replaced by sophisticated electronic monitoring devices. The newborn was no longer considered a small child, but a new type of patient, the neonate, which created a new type of medicine—neonatology. Premature babies and newborns with problems were now receiving medical care in Neonatal Intensive Care Units

(NICU), which were manned by a new breed of pediatricians known as neonatologists.

In obstetrics, new concepts were being introduced: high-risk obstetrics, high-risk patients, and maternal fetal medicine. A new breed of obstetricians, known as maternal fetal medicine specialists, were taking over the care of newly defined "high-risk pregnancies."

Pediatricians who wanted to care for newborns, and obstetricians who wanted to care for high-risk mothers and fetuses had to obtain additional training and become certified as neonatologists or maternal fetal medicine specialists.

Depending on their capability of caring for complicated obstetrical patients and their babies, hospitals were now labeled as Level 1, Level 2 or Level 3. High-risk regional centers were established, depending on the number of deliveries, services available, and the presence or absence of maternal fetal medicine specialists and neonatologists on their staff. One can say, without exaggeration, that from 1960 on, a revolution occurred in obstetrical and neonatal care. Smaller and smaller babies were being born prematurely and surviving. Mothers who before could not have dreamed of attempting pregnancy without risking their lives, were now the happy mothers of healthy children. One of the most revolutionary advances in obstetrical care was the ability to see the fetus by way of ultrasound, and to treat the baby inside the womb. Such interventions are saving babies from an inexorable death before birth. The baby inside the womb became a new entity: the fetus as a patient.

By the beginning of the twenty-first century, obstetrical and neonatal care were as far from eighteenth-century midwifery as the horse and buggy were from supersonic aviation. Obstetricians who used to arrive at the hospital minutes before a laboring woman delivered, if they arrived in time at all, now spend hours in the labor and delivery area. Practices with multiple physicians now have a call schedule, where one obstetrician is in the hospital twenty-four hours a day. Maternal fetal medicine specialists are mostly hospital-based physicians, as are neonatologists, and are in the hospital at all times on a rotation basis.

Nurses in the labor and delivery area and the operating room nurses are now specialized in the care of high-risk obstetrical patients. This specialization has led to other specialties involved in the care of pregnant women. For example, we have now obstetrical anesthesiologists, who also have to care for two patients: the mother and her unborn baby.

Maternal mortality in the US has decreased from 850 in 100,000 births in 1900 to 12.7 in 100,000 births in 2010: this is still too high, but it is a dramatic improvement. The lowest maternal mortality in the US was recorded in 1982, when it was 7.5 in 100,000. The reason for its recent increase is still unclear. Nowadays, even extremely premature infants of barely one pound have been known to survive. Maternal diseases like diabetes no longer threaten a woman's life if she becomes pregnant. Treating the baby before its birth, including surgery before birth, is common and is saving many babies who otherwise would have died.

We now understand that time is always of the essence in an obstetrical emergency. It used to be that all cesarean sections were performed in the general surgery unit, which was usually away from the labor and delivery area. Sometimes, all surgical operating rooms were busy and one would have to wait a long time for a room to become available. Anesthesiologists treated the mother as a surgical patient, and paid little attention to the fetus.

Now it is rare for any major US hospital not to have surgical operating rooms right in the labor and delivery area. These are never used for any other surgery, except for obstetrical surgeries. There are usually two surgical rooms, so two cesarean sections can be performed at the same time, if necessary.

As chief of a university obstetrical service during my career, we instituted emergency drills not unlike fire drills. The purpose of such drills was to minimize the time it would take to have a pregnant patient in the operating room and ready for surgery. We were able to reduce that time from forty-five minutes to just twelve minutes. Once an obstetrical emergency was called, the operating room was ready for surgery. The obstetrical nurses would wheel the patient to the operating room and have her on the operating table. Anesthesia and neonatology services would be in the operating room, and the surgeon would have washed, gowned and gloved, ready to operate. A good surgeon would be able to have a baby delivered by cesarean section in a further three minutes, therefore delivering the baby in the quickest possible time in emergency conditions.

Looking back at the history of such progress makes us all feel proud. Our work, however, is far from over. Maternal deaths are still too high. They absolutely have to be reduced to an irreducible minimum. Historically, the three main causes of maternal deaths were hemorrhage, hypertension (preeclampsia/eclampsia), and infections. These three causes are still claiming the lives of mothers-to-be today. Prematurity is still the most common cause of neonatal deaths. Prevention of prematurity is another prime goal in current efforts to improve obstetrical care. Until such time as our statistics improve, we should not claim victory, and we cannot rest until a reduction in maternal and fetal mortality is achieved.

"I can't be pregnant—I'm on the pill!"

Throughout history, women have always attempted to control their fertility, both in terms of getting pregnant as well as avoiding pregnancy. In the second century, the Greek physician Soranus taught that women were fertile during ovulation, but missed the mark by believing that ovulation occurred during menstruation. It was known from antiquity that a nursing mother rarely became pregnant. Withdrawal method (coitus interruptus), as a fertility control, is even mentioned in the Bible.

Over time, many attempts were made to find the perfect birth control method. From crocodile dung, to olive oil, tobacco juice, ginger, douches, sea sponges and many others, all had their proponents and believers. Condoms first made an appearance around 1300 BC, by the eighteenth century, they were commonplace, made of sausage skins. Yet, it was not until 1921 that Margaret Sanger opened the first birth control clinic in Brooklyn, New York.

The second half of the twentieth century was marked by a social and scientific revolution in regards to the ability of a woman to control her fertility. Unlike other medical advances, fertility control was not considered a medical advance, but a moral and religious issue. As such, ethical debates on the subject were vigorous. The "pill" became available to the public by 1960, but was not legal everywhere. In 1965, the case of *Griswold v the State of Connecticut* reached the Supreme Court. At the time, the State considered the sale of the pill illegal, but the Supreme Court ruled that married people were entitled to use contraception, and that making it a crime to sell birth control was unconstitutional. At about the same time, the feminist movement was in full swing, its roots dating back to the earlier suffragette movement that fought for women's right to vote. By the late sixties, the feminist movement was concerned with political, cultural, and economic inequalities, and women's right to self-determination, which included the right for women to make their own decisions regarding pregnancy. Birth control, of course, was one of the issues.

By the turn of the twenty-first century, birth control, primarily the pill, was widely accepted and used; however, even today, the Catholic Church opposes any form of contraception with the exception of the rhythm method, which is based on avoiding intercourse during and around ovulation. Regardless, a woman of reproductive age who does not use, at one time or another, some form of contraception is rare. Despite its popularity, I was always surprised at how little information patients received when requesting the pill for birth control. In my experience, one in three women probably had little understanding of how the pill worked, what the risks were, or how to use it correctly. Unfortunately, health professionals generally provide only cursory information about it, and take their patient's basic knowledge of contraception for granted. Consequently, misuse of the pill is not uncommon. But I must say that, even for me, Helen's story was unique.

Helen was referred to my office by another physician. She was forty years old, was taking birth control pills, and had missed two periods in a row. She had talked to her physician, who was not an obstetrician, and he thought that perhaps she might be pregnant and suggested she see me as soon as possible.

The first thing she told me when I entered the room was: "I can't be pregnant; I am on birth control pills." Of course, it was not the first time I had seen a patient who had become pregnant while on birth control pills. Usually, there was a simple explanation—she missed a pill or two, she changed the type of birth control pills she was taking in the middle of a cycle, she started her pill cycle late, or some other reason. In Helen's case, however, because of her age and the fact that the pregnancy was only suspected, it was indeed likely that she was not pregnant. Missed periods, in themselves, are not always caused by pregnancy.

Helen already had four children. She had been married for twenty years. After the birth of her fourth child, she and her husband had decided their family was complete and she had started taking birth control pills. While she was on the pill, her periods became irregular. Bleeding would occur more than once a month and at irregular intervals. Helen's irregular bleeding was non-standard for a woman taking birth control pills. While taking the pill, women should have periods once a month.

After taking her medical history, I proceeded with a physical examination. Helen was a healthy, normal lady. Her pelvic examination, however, was distinctly consistent with an intrauterine pregnancy, which I estimated at about twelve weeks. Telling her she was pregnant would not have achieved much at that time, since she was adamant she was not. I suggested we perform an ultrasound, to which she agreed.

I positioned the ultrasound screen in such a way so as to be visible to us both, and I started by looking at the upper abdomen. Slowly, I approached the pelvis in the lower abdomen. As soon as the ultrasonic beam was on top of the uterus, the baby appeared clearly on the screen, moving around inside the uterus.
Before I could say anything, Helen screamed, "Oh my God, what is that?"
"That's a baby," I said. "You are indeed pregnant."

She started crying uncontrollably. For the first time, I felt uncomfortable, not knowing what to say. I could certainly understand how, at age forty, with the knowledge she had completed her family, pregnancy might not be what a woman like Helen would have in mind.
"I don't believe this … we were always so careful to take the pill every day…"
"What do you mean 'we'?" I asked.
"Well," she said, "…my husband and I. Some evenings I would take the pill, and sometimes, he would take the pill. We never missed a day."
I suggested that she get dressed and join me in the office to discuss it.

During my years of practice, I heard many unusual stories, but Helen's was a new twist. It would have been funny, were it not that I felt sorry for Helen. Sometimes, physicians think their instructions to the patient are clearly understood when they may not be, and I came to thinking that often we consider certain information self-evident when it is not always so. We forget far too often that "doctor" means "teacher." In a busy practice, we tend to give quick, basic information instead of teaching. Helen's case was typical of a physician who assumed certain things were obvious; only, to Helen at least, they were not.

By the time Helen joined me in the office, she had calmed down a lot, although my Kleenex box still came in handy. She told me she had been on the pill since the birth of her last child, five years ago. She had been given a prescription and some cursory instructions about potential problems. How did she start sharing the pill with her husband, and why?
"I got tired of taking a pill every day, and we thought it would not make any difference as long as he was taking the pill when I was not."
It sounded almost logical. Did she consult with her physician? No. They had lost their health insurance for a while, and she started attending a clinic where her prescription was regularly renewed. She usually had a cursory visit once a year when she had a Pap smear. Even when they had health insurance again, she continued with the clinic for her birth control pills and yearly Pap smear. Did she ever read the instructions the pharmacist usually includes with the prescription? No.

I explained to Helen how taking pills irregularly would cause irregular bleeding (which we call breakthrough bleeding), how the pill actually works, and why she got pregnant. In fact, I was surprised that she had not become pregnant earlier.

Helen was speechless. Then she said, "I don't know what to say. I feel so embarrassed."
I made the point to tell her that sometimes silly things happen. Sometimes, we take it for granted that we know something so obvious, when in reality we missed the point.
"Charles, my husband, will be shocked," she added.

Helen became my patient and had an uncomplicated pregnancy. She delivered a healthy boy. After delivery, she did not wish to use birth control pills again and had a postpartum tubal ligation.

* * *

I don't want to know

Over the past thirty years, the practice of obstetrics has changed significantly, primarily due to technological advances that have improved our ability to see and treat the baby long before its birth. The most important of these technologies was ultrasound. The use of ultrasound allows us to actually visualize the baby inside the uterus, to determine if there are any gross abnormalities, and to follow the baby's growth and development. In some circumstances, under ultrasonographic guidance, we can even medically treat the baby. Even before their birth, babies can now successfully undergo certain surgical procedures or receive blood transfusions. Ultrasound also allows us to refine our evaluation of the child's well-being, by determining whether the cord blood flows adequately or not. A normal cord blood flow is always a sign of baby's well-being. We are also able to look for and analyze the infant's activity to draw conclusions about its health and comfort. An infant who moves vigorously is a healthy baby. The newest development is the visualization of the baby in 3-D, which provides outstanding, almost photographic, images of the infant.

Ultrasound gives parents the opportunity to see their baby or find out its sex, if they so desire. Some are eager to find out, but others prefer to be surprised. In many circumstances, the mere fact that they can see their baby may be reassuring, particularly if they have concerns about the baby, or if they are just anxious.

Today, it is routine for all pregnant women to have an ultrasound study at their first office visit. This is done not only to determine whether there are any abnormalities, but also to establish when delivery is to be expected. Ultrasound in early pregnancy is a very accurate way to estimate the delivery date, since estimating the due date based on the last menstrual period is not always reliable. Later in pregnancy, when variations between babies of the same gestational age may be significant, determining due date becomes more unreliable.

Parents also look forward to this early ultrasound, when they can see their baby for the first time. The majority of parents want to learn the sex of their baby, but sometimes parents may not always agree. That was the case with Cecilia and her husband.

Cecilia came to my office at the suggestion of her family physician. As a child, she had rheumatic fever, and as a consequence, one of her heart valves was damaged. She had been, however, asymptomatic, and her cardiologist told her she would tolerate pregnancy well. Cecilia was sixteen weeks pregnant with her first pregnancy when she came to see me.

She was in good general health. Her cardiologist's written evaluation, which she brought with her, told me that one of her valves was minimally affected and that she had no symptoms whatsoever. All of her other valves were fine, which was reassuring. I concurred with her cardiologist that she should tolerate pregnancy well.

Part of my examination was to obtain an ultrasound, which confirmed she was indeed about sixteen weeks pregnant. Both Cecilia and her husband, Tom, were delighted with being able to see their infant for the first time. During the ultrasound, I asked them if they would like to know the sex of the baby. Cecilia immediately said, "No, I want to be surprised."
Tom, however, said, "Well, don't tell her, but I want to know."

That was unusual. Parents usually decide whether they want to know their infant's sex long before they reach the doctor's office. I did not remember the last time I had encountered a disagreement between mother and father in that respect.
"I am sorry, Tom," I said, "but Cecilia is my patient, and if she does not want to know the sex of the infant, I cannot tell anyone, not even you."
Tom looked at me, stunned. "What do you mean you can't tell me? I am the father."
"That's true, but your wife does not want to know, so I am bound by whatever she wants me to do in this regard. She is my patient, and we respect our patients' wishes," I replied.

"Leave me alone with my wife for a moment, please?"
I told them I would gladly do so and offered for them to use my office so they could be more comfortable. Tom did not want any part of that, and said, "Here is fine."

I left the examining room. Tom, apparently, was very upset. I could hear his voice through the closed door. They must have been alone for about ten minutes when Tom suddenly walked out of the room, slammed the door, and left the area without saying a word. When I returned, Cecilia was sobbing alone in the room. I explained to her that I would abide by her decision, but I could not tell her husband without her permission. If she would like to sign a release allowing me to tell her husband, I would do so.

Cecilia apologized for the incident. She told me they had argued about it at home before coming to the office, but she absolutely did not want to know the infant's sex until he or she was born. She thanked me for not letting them know the sex of the baby. She had not expected a scene in my office, but obviously Tom had other ideas. Cecilia made an appointment for the next visit, and she left the office. About ten minutes later, she returned. She told the nurse that her husband had actually left and as she had no transportation, she needed to call a cab. The nurse came and told me what had happened. I asked the nurse if perhaps she could drive Cecilia home, to which she readily agreed.

I felt sorry for Cecilia; the infant's sex argument appeared to me to be symptomatic of some serious problems. Cecilia continued to see me during her pregnancy, but Tom never accompanied her again. The next time I saw him was at the delivery. Cecilia had a healthy seven-pound girl.

Does genetic screening have all the answers?

When I started out as an obstetrician, prenatal testing was not available, but now, highly accurate screening and diagnosis can be performed early in pregnancy. Scientifically, this was a tremendous breakthrough. When certain abnormalities, other than chromosomal, are detected, it allows us, in some cases, to treat the infant before its birth. Prenatal testing for chromosomal abnormalities, on the other hand, can create a heartbreaking situation for the parents, both morally and emotionally. In such cases, they will be facing one of the most difficult decisions of their lives.

For Betty and Jim, an unplanned pregnancy forced them to choose what tests Betty should have—if any—and how they would proceed if problems were uncovered. Looking for common ground was not easy.

Betty and Jim were teachers and the parents of two children, an eight-year-old girl and a six-year-old boy. Betty's pregnancy took them by surprise. They were not planning on having any more children. Betty, who was now thirty-five, was fourteen weeks pregnant when she and Jim came to see me.

You probably don't think a thirty-five-year-old woman is of "advanced" age, but in obstetrics, women thirty-five or older are known as AMA, or Advanced Maternal Age. That's when doctors start considering the risk of chromosomal abnormalities in the baby is significant. It is also when doctors typically begin recommending genetic diagnostic tests. That was why Betty and Jim had come to see me: their doctor had suggested genetic counseling and screening tests because of Betty's "advanced" age.

Many obstetricians consider genetic screening as simply a statistical decision-making process; I don't agree. It is an emotional decision with profound implications for both parents. Numbers give parents data, but not answers.

What are some of the numbers that come into play during genetic screening? Women of any age can conceive a child with chromosomal abnormalities. However, the risk increases as women grow older. For example, the risk for Down syndrome jumps from 1 in 1,667 at age twenty, to 1 in 30 at age forty-five. At thirty-five, Betty's age-based risk was 1 in 385. These numbers are based only on age-related statistics.

In circumstances like that, the question that parents must answer is, first of all, whether they even want to know if their baby has a chromosomal abnormality. This is not as simple as it sounds. In the event that a couple wants to know, they have to understand that if the news is bad, there is no available treatment to correct a chromosomal abnormality. Furthermore, the tests that provide the most accurate information are both invasive procedures, which have their own risks. One is a CVS, or chorionic villus sampling, which is performed very early in pregnancy, usually before the twelfth week. The other is an amniocentesis, performed later in pregnancy, somewhere between fifteen and eighteen weeks gestation. The purpose of both of these tests is to obtain some fetal tissue in order to be able to perform a chromosomal study. In the case of CVS, a small piece of placenta is retrieved. In amniocentesis, amniotic fluid, in which fetal cells are present, is obtained.

In CVS, a fine catheter is guided through the vagina and cervix, and inside the uterus to the edge of the placenta. To perform an amniocentesis, a needle is placed through the abdomen inside the uterus, and amniotic fluid is retrieved. Both of these procedures are invasive, and carry the risks of a miscarriage. In the US, according to the Centers for Disease Control and Prevention (CDC) the risk of an amniocentesis complication is about 1 in 400, while for CVS it is about 1 in 200-300. Thus, it is conceivable that by attempting to find out about a potential problem with the baby, an otherwise perfectly healthy pregnancy may be lost. These two tests are the only ones that, at this time, give us an absolute answer.

Other, non-invasive tests can also provide percentages that are broader in scope than just the mother's age. One such test is known as the "quad screen." This is a blood test that measures the levels of four substances—two hormones and two proteins—in the mother's blood. The results of a quad screen can raise or lower the statistical age-related likelihood that the baby may have genetic abnormalities. Normal results lower those risks, and abnormal results raise it. But this test still cannot tell us for sure whether genetic chromosomal problems exist. Should a quad screen be reported as abnormal, doctors usually recommend an amniocentesis.

Not everyone is willing to have an amniocentesis, not only because of the miscarriage risk, but because nothing can be done to treat a baby who has abnormal chromosomes. All that doctors can offer parents is the choice of whether to continue the pregnancy and deliver a child with genetic abnormalities, or end the pregnancy. Those who would not consider abortion as an option often don't even start down the path to genetic testing. Others do, even though they would not end the pregnancy, because it gives them a few months to prepare for the birth of a special-needs child.

This was where Betty and Jim found themselves. Although they both opposed abortion, Betty wanted to go through with the genetic testing. Jim did not. I wanted to offer some perspective that might help them make a decision with which they could both feel comfortable. I explained the concept of risk. Risk is a statistical possibility. Based on nothing more than Betty's age, her risk of having a child with chromosomal abnormalities was 1 in 385. To most couples, that sounds like a big risk, but it also means that 384 out of 385 women will not have a baby with chromosomal abnormalities. So, for Betty, the likelihood of having a chromosomally normal baby was 99.74%. The same information when presented in a different way puts the risk into perspective and makes it appear less extreme.

Having a better understanding of their risks, Jim and Betty both seemed relieved, but unfortunately, their feelings about testing did not change. Betty wanted it, and Jim did not. I suggested they go home and think about it.

They returned to my office a few days later. As soon as I entered the room, I could feel the tension between them. I greeted them both and asked if they had reached a decision.

"Go ahead," Betty said to Jim.

"I already told you," Jim answered, "it's your baby, you decide."

Betty and Jim were at an impasse, something that happens fairly frequently. Pregnancy is the result of a partnership, but that doesn't mean both partners feel the same about decisions involving the pregnancy. Compromises have to be made, but because having a baby is such an emotional event, people often struggle to find common ground. Sometimes, faced with uncertainty, the husband disengages himself and assigns all of the responsibility to his wife. I had seen this situation many times before, but I was surprised Jim had taken this approach. They seemed like a very well-adjusted couple.

Betty started to cry. Jim fidgeted in his chair. "I don't know why you want to go through with this screening," he told her. "If the baby has a problem, we both agreed you won't have an abortion."

"If the baby has a problem, I want to know and be prepared," Betty explained. "I don't want to be surprised in the delivery room."

I felt encouraged by this exchange. I have seen couples where one parent would choose abortion if the baby was abnormal, while the other would not. At other times, couples engage in a genetic "blame game," finger-pointing over whose fault a genetic problem might be. In Jim and Betty's case, since neither would opt for abortion, theirs was more a procedural difference than a fundamental ethical issue. But it was still a problem without an apparent solution.

As a physician, I must remain neutral in situations like this. But I can give a perspective that helps couples come to a decision, and that's what I tried to do with Betty and Jim. I reminded Betty that when she had been pregnant with her second child, six years earlier at age twenty-nine, her age-related statistical risk of having a baby with Down syndrome had been about 1 in 1,000.

"True," she said, "but I didn't know that then."

"If you had known, would you have gone through genetic screening or diagnosis?"

After a pause she said, "Probably not." In other words, with a 1 in 1,000 risk, Betty would feel comfortable not having an amniocentesis.

In this pregnancy, Betty was starting out with a baseline risk of 1 in 385. A quad screen would either lower or raise those numbers, so I suggested she have the quad screen. If it changed her risk for the better, Betty would feel satisfied. If it changed it for the worse, she may consider an amniocentesis, or she may not.

Betty and Jim both agreed to this. As it turned out, the numbers were on their side. Betty's quad screen blood test showed a risk of 1 in 7,400—much better than her original age-based risk. Betty and Jim were both pleased and did not pursue any further genetic testing. Her pregnancy was uncomplicated, and Betty delivered an eight pound, one ounce little girl.

I am sick every morning

Everyone has heard of "morning sickness," that awful time in
early pregnancy when nausea and vomiting seem to take over a
woman's life. It happens in some women, but not all, and it usually
just goes away as the pregnancy continues. However, sometimes
it doesn't. When it does not subside on its own, obstetricians
call it "hyperemesis gravidarum." It occurs when the nausea and
vomiting become uncontrollable and constant, and the patient may
require hospitalization.

Now, you may wonder, what causes this? We really don't know.
Some people think it is due to genetic factors, or some kind of
hormonal imbalance. Unspoken family problems may sometimes
be a factor. Psychological factors, when present, may turn serious
and psychiatric treatment may become necessary. But the truth is:
we don't know.

When Kim and David walked into my office, I was surprised at
how young they were. They were recently married, and Kim was
eight weeks pregnant. They both wanted a large family, so this
was the beginning of that journey for them. They had a gazillion
questions regarding what happens during pregnancy. I could tell
from their enthusiasm that this young couple was bursting at the
seams with the excitement of prospective parenthood.

Kim was eighteen and healthy. After her initial exam, and based
upon her history, I fully expected she would have an uncomplicated
pregnancy. We discussed prenatal vitamins, her diet, and all of the
dos and don'ts. I scheduled her next appointment for the following
month.

A few days later, Kim called to tell me she had been suffering a
lot of nausea and vomiting. Since morning sickness is common in
early pregnancy, I reassured her there was nothing to be worried
about and gave her some basic instructions about eating small
portions, eating only what was appealing, and maybe having some
ice cream. If vomiting became a problem, she was to let me know

and we would try some medication to help control her nausea. My instinct told me that she just had a mild case of pregnancy-related nausea and vomiting.

A few days later, her husband called me. He was distraught and concerned. Kim was still vomiting and not feeling well. I asked him to bring Kim in to my office. Once in the office, I decided to proceed with an ultrasound. Seeing the baby moving and its heart beating is always reassuring to both mother and father. Under the circumstance, I thought it was important to reassure them of the baby's well-being. It also allowed me to visualize the pregnancy and confirm that everything appeared fine. During the ultrasound examination, which I purposely prolonged, Kim had no uncontrollable vomiting or nausea. She had not had any on the way to the office either. In addition, she did not look sick, she did not appear dehydrated, and basically, her vital signs and examination were normal. That was reassuring to me. My impression was that she was doing well and I did not feel that medical intervention, other than reassurance, was needed.

A week later, Kim called the office and requested to talk to me. She told me she would like to see me in private, as soon as possible. We made arrangements for her to visit that same afternoon.

In my office, we talked at length about a multitude of problems. She showed no signs of nausea during our conversation. Sometimes, plain distraction improves the condition, and in this case, leaving the house, being in the office and chatting for a long time, was enough to focus her attention on something other than her vomiting. I explained this to Kim and reassured her that she would do well in her pregnancy despite the unpleasantness of the nausea and vomiting.

She surprised met by stating, "I don't think so."
After a moment, I asked, "Is there something you know that I do not?"
Her response was immediate and emphatic. "Yes," she said. "My mother-in-law is driving me crazy." She proceeded to tell me that they shared an apartment complex with her in-laws, and therefore

her mother-in-law was constantly in Kim's apartment. Her mother-in-law was a very domineering woman, telling her what to do and what not to do during pregnancy, how she planned to take care of her grandchild, and a multitude of other "suggestions" that irritated Kim. Furthermore, Kim's husband was not supportive and was playing mama's boy instead of assuming the role of a protective husband.

"I have reached the point," she said, "where, at the mere sight of her, I have a lump in my stomach. I get nauseated and invariably end up vomiting."

Kim's statement went right to the root of the problem. I felt sorry for her. During my career, I saw many times the impact family problems can have on a pregnant woman. What's more, if this were to continue, Kim might continue to have a very rough time unless she were able to take control of the situation.

My concern was Kim's well-being. Experience told me that what began as a nuisance could become a real problem. I tried to find out more about her husband's role in this family situation, but Kim obviously preferred not to talk about it. I voiced my concern and indicated to Kim that this constant nausea and vomiting may turn into a serious medical problem, and that her pregnancy was not the cause of it. I emphasized the consequences if she continued on this path of psychological, uncontrollable vomiting. I was perfectly willing to have Kim and David come to my office together and talk about it, but she opted to take care of it herself.

I did not hear from Kim for about a week or so, so I thought that, hopefully, she had succeeded in improving her relationship with her mother-in-law. That was not the case.

Ten days after her earlier visit to my office, at around three o'clock in the morning, I was awakened by a call from our emergency room physician. He promptly told me that an ambulance had brought Kim there. Apparently, she had collapsed while on the way to the bathroom in the middle of the night. She was dehydrated and weak. Her laboratory results were still pending, but I told him I was on my way to the hospital.

31

When I got there, in addition to her husband, an older couple was with Kim in the room. David introduced them as his parents. I greeted them and asked if they could please wait in the waiting room. David's mother immediately objected and said she wanted to be by her daughter-in-law's side. As courteously as I could, I firmly told her that, at this time, she was to sit in the waiting room. I also asked David if he would wait with his parents, to which he promptly agreed. He stood and took his parents with him to the waiting area.

Kim was able to tell me that, after she last saw me, she had confronted her mother in-law, which had not helped. Furthermore, her husband had told her she was childish and that his mother only wanted to help. For the past week, Kim had suffered nausea and vomiting. She had been feeling weak, but thought it due to not eating. That evening, when she had woken up to go to the bathroom, she had felt dizzy and passed out.

My examination reassured me that Kim had not hurt herself in the fall, but the laboratory results indicated the constant vomiting was beginning to take its toll on her. Some of her blood chemistries were borderline or abnormal. The emergency room physicians had already started intravenous fluids. Correcting her blood chemistry would not be a problem. I also performed an ultrasound on her to ensure that the baby was doing well. I told Kim she would be admitted into the hospital and that she would be allowed no visitors for the time being—that included her family. She whispered, "Thank you."

Back in the waiting room, I told the family about my decision. As expected, her mother in-law confronted me about not allowing any visitors. I told her my decision was in Kim's best interests. Until such a time as I was satisfied that Kim's condition had improved, no visitors would be allowed. Part of the therapy, I told her mother-in-law, includes complete rest for Kim, no exceptions. Then I asked David to please come with me.

We went into one of the little conference rooms in the emergency room area. I needed to talk to him so that he understood the problem. David was probably no more than twenty-two or twenty-three years old. From the little I knew of his behavior in this situation, I assumed he was a little immature. I had to take the bull by the horns if my patient—his wife—was to enjoy her pregnancy. I started talking to him in as simple terms as I possibly could, to make sure he understood exactly what his wife was going through.

His concerned look slowly began changing into one of bewilderment. He never interrupted me, but at one point, he asked, "Why didn't she tell me?"
"Maybe you did not hear," I answered.

A remarkable transformation took place in this young man over the course of our conversation. He was no longer the same person who followed me into that room. It was clear that he suddenly realized he had responsibilities, that he had a family over and beyond that of his parents, that he was going to be a father, and that the mother of his future child was sick and that he could do something about that. He stood up without saying a word, and then looked at me for some time. "Could I see my wife now, for just a minute?" he asked. "Most certainly." I replied.
He extended his hand and said, "Thank you, sir." We shook hands and he left the room.

I made arrangements for Kim to be hospitalized and wrote the necessary orders. When I was finished, I returned to the waiting room. Neither David nor his parents were there. I went to Kim's room. David was sitting next to Kim's bed, holding her hand. I told Kim I would see her in the morning and suggested that David go home and get some rest.

Kim remained in the hospital for a few days. My "no visitors" order was not challenged again during her stay. She started eating a little bit at a time, and when discharged she felt confident that the worse was over.

Kim came to see me four days after she left hospital. I was pleased to see she was doing well, and that she was again the happy young lady I had met at her first visit.

What are we going to do?

Mary was in her third pregnancy. The previous two pregnancies
had ended in miscarriages very early in pregnancy, so her
obstetrician had suggested she consult me in view of her previous
two losses. Both had occurred before the seventh week of
pregnancy, with no apparent cause.

Mary was only twenty-five years old. When I first saw her, she
was already eighteen weeks pregnant. Other than the miscarriages,
she was healthy, as was her husband. Since both losses occurred
before the seventh week, having reached now eighteen weeks was
reassuring to both Mary and me.

I asked if she would mind us proceeding with an ultrasound, to
which she readily agreed. Both Mary and Justin were excited to
see their infant moving around and to see the heartbeat of the baby.
Immediately, they asked me if I could tell the infant's sex. It was a
boy, which made them very happy. Unfortunately, this was not the
end of the story.

The infant had an abdominal wall defect—a hole through which
bowel loops extruded to float freely in the amniotic fluid. This
abnormality is known as gastroschisis, and is not an unusual
malformation. Usually, it is not associated with chromosomal
abnormalities or any other malformation. After birth, the infant
undergoes a surgical procedure to replace the bowel loops in the
abdomen and the abdominal wall is repaired. I explained this to
Mary and Justin.

Mary started crying. "I don't believe this," she said. "First, two
miscarriages, and now this." Justin was trying to console her,
but was not doing a very good job. I asked them to join me in my
office. Once we sat down, I repeated my explanation of what we
had found, emphasizing the good prognosis for this baby.
"How can we be sure that it's going to be ok?" asked Justin.
"We can never be sure of anything," I told them. "However, we
make judgment calls based on our experience, as well as on that

of other people." I reemphasized that infants with gastroschisis do well in the vast majority of cases, so while this finding was unexpected, it is far from tragic. I told them that after surgery, and as the baby grows, the only thing that will remind them of this would be a small scar.

I had the distinct feeling that neither Mary nor Justin were registering what I was saying. I asked them if they truly understood what we were dealing with.
"Yes," Mary said, "the baby is malformed. Didn't you say that?"
"No. What I said is that the baby has a malformation; I did not say that it is malformed."
Mary continued to cry and I had the feeling that Justin did not know what to do. He seemed a little more composed, but I was not sure.

We kept talking for some time, but we were making little progress. The only thing Mary had registered was that her baby was malformed and I was beginning to be unsure what Justin had registered. I decided my best bet would be to give them some literature and general information about gastroschisis, and ask them to return in a week to talk some more, during which time I would try to answer whatever questions they had. I also reminded them that chromosomal diagnostic testing was available, should they so decide.

When they returned to the office, they seemed more composed—at first. Their questions, however, soon became surprising. Justin's first question was: "Will he be able to play football?" It took me by surprise. Was he kidding or what? "I can't tell if any kid will be able to play football just by the way they look before birth," I answered. "Is that your main concern?"
"No, I was just wondering," he said, kind of apologetically.
Mary wanted to know if his brain would be affected.
"He won't be retarded because he has a gastroschisis," I replied. I told her gastroschisis only affects the gut, not the brain.
"What are we supposed to tell our family?" Mary continued. "We never had such a problem in our families."

SILVIO ALADJEM MD

I knew we were not going anywhere with this line of questioning. These were two intelligent people; their reaction, however, was unusual to say the least. They obviously had a major problem accepting that their infant had an abnormality. I decided I would have to start all over again and try to discover what was behind their reaction. It just wasn't right.

"Look," I said, "if there is any consolation, quite a few parents have faced the reality that their child may not be perfect. Nothing in life is perfect. But explain to me why are you concerned about what to say to your family? Why can't you tell them the truth, assuming you want to tell them anything? Why are you concerned about whether the child will play football or not? I need to understand where you are coming from if I am to help you."

Mary started crying and sobbing. She told me how much she wanted a child, but a normal child. No one in her family had ever had an abnormal child. What was she going to do? How could she tell her parents, her family or her friends that she was going to have an abnormal baby?
I reminded her that after surgery this child would be normal. She should stop thinking of him as abnormal.
"Are you absolutely sure?" she said.
"No," I replied. "I do not play God. I can only tell you what my experience, and other's experiences, have been. If you want 100% assurance, I cannot give it to you any more than I can assure you that you will not have a car accident on the way home. Frankly," I continued, "you give me the impression you are more concerned about what family and friends are going to say than about how the infant is going to do. Think about it."

Justin was silent. There was a long pause until he started talking. "Doc," he said, "the problem is that, for quite some time, Mary could not get pregnant." After this introduction, he loosened up and told me how much the family had been pressuring them to see a doctor about her inability to conceive. They had not been able to afford to do that, but when she finally became pregnant—when they least expected it—they were happy. Unfortunately, she had a

36

miscarriage, and then a second one. The family pressure increased, particularly from Mary's family, who had made her feel like the ugly duckling of the family. When she got pregnant for the third time, they had kept it secret from the family, but as the pregnancy went on, they told them. The fact that this baby had a problem had created a tremendous amount of stress, for obvious reasons. It was not that they did not care; they were just overwhelmed.

I thanked him for his frankness; at least now I could understand. My suggestion was that they consider family counseling. I suggested that there were counselors available who may help them cope with the situation better than I could. Or, they could decide that this, after all, was their baby, and they could choose to confront the family in any way they felt worked for them. Pregnancies are very personal, each with its own untold problems. Ultimately, it is exclusively the couple's choice what, how or when to do what they need to do. It is no one else's business, any more than raising a child is.

Mary had stopped crying, and Justin seemed to have taken a load off his chest. He finally told me that they would do what needed to be done. Then he added, "I am sorry for my silly question; I don't know what I was thinking."
I told him not to worry; that I understood.

Mary and Justin came back two weeks later for her regular visit, at which I performed an ultrasound. Mary pointed to the screen and said, "Look, Justin, the baby's heart—it's beating."
I purposely kept the screen steady for them at that point. Then I showed them the eyes, the nose, the head, the arms moving, and the hand in a fist. I even showed them that it was a boy. Mary asked me to point to the bowels of the infant, and I did.
"Could I have a picture of my baby showing the bowels out?" she asked. "I will be happy to do that for you," I said. I thought, *She won't have any problems anymore*, and I was pleased.

When can she get pregnant again?

At about eight o'clock one night, I received a call from the emergency room physician. He had just admitted a young woman who was about two months pregnant and bleeding. She'd had no prenatal care and had no personal primary physician. Furthermore, she had suffered seven previous miscarriages. The ER physician rightly classified her as a high-risk patient, and therefore he had called me. I told him I was on my way.

When I arrived, the charge nurse told me the patient was bleeding moderately and was having some cramping, but that, right now, all of her labs were within accepted limits. I thanked her and went directly to the patient, whose name was Ashley. She was twenty-five years old and was accompanied by her boyfriend, James.

Ashley was crying softly. Based on her last menstrual period dates, she was barely two months pregnant. She had apparently started bleeding that evening, first spotting, and subsequently bleeding heavily, as if at the beginning of a period. I could hardly believe it when she told me, "This is my eighth pregnancy. We have lost seven pregnancies in three years. I cannot believe I am losing this one too. It is just more than I can take."
Ashley did not know why she had lost seven pregnancies. I talked to her some more and she told me she desperately wanted a baby and that she had actually refused any testing or examinations after her previous miscarriages.

It was then that her boyfriend, James, spoke up. "We don't want to waste any time with expensive medical tests."
I was surprised by what he had said. This was another new situation for me. How could anyone lose seven babies and not want to know why? There were some serious issues going on here that I just had to discover. It is common to see a patient with two or three miscarriages who has made little attempt to find the cause, but this was the first time I had ever had been faced with seven miscarriages in three years and no information as to why.

Ashley was otherwise healthy. She denied being diabetic, a common cause for repeated miscarriages, or having a family history of diabetes. She had two sisters, both of which had children and neither of whom had experienced any miscarriages.

I asked the nurse to please bring me the portable ultrasound equipment and to prepare Ashley for a pelvic examination. When the nurse left the examining room, Ashley started complaining of severe cramping. Immediately thereafter, she followed with a gush of fluid and vaginal bleeding. It was obvious to me she was in the process of aborting her pregnancy. When the nurse returned, I was able to examine Ashley. Her cervix was open and pieces of placental tissue were found in the vagina.

I explained to Ashley and James that she was aborting, and that I would have to perform dilation and curettage in order to remove any remaining tissue. Subsequently, I called the operating room and told them that Ashley was on her way and that I would carry out a D & C as soon as an anesthesiologist was available. James could accompany Ashley all the way to the operating room area, I told him to wait in the family waiting room. I would come to talk to him once I completed the procedure.

As I strode towards the operating room area, I tried to understand what was going on with Ashley. Seven pregnancies in three years is certainly not the norm. Why wouldn't she want to find out what's wrong? What was behind her story? I was also troubled by her boyfriend's behavior. Throughout my interaction with Ashley, the only comment he had made was about the high cost of medical testing—the reason they had not pursued further investigation into the cause of his girlfriend's miscarriages. It bothered me that not once had he expressed any interest in Ashley's well-being or her condition. It was certainly not what we usually see in obstetrics. Hopefully, further discussion with both Ashley and her boyfriend would provide the answers I was seeking.

Once I got to the operating room, the head nurse told me that the anesthesiologist, Dr. Murphy, would be available immediately.

She went on to ask whether the chart note was correct: was this Ashley's eighth miscarriage in three years, or had there been a typo. I told her there was no typo; the information was correct.

"Oh my," she said, and then added, "You'll be in room two. We'll bring the patient right away." It was evident I was not the only one thinking that something very wrong was going on.

I proceeded to scrub and then entered the operating room. By then, Ashley was on the operating table. Dr. Murphy was preparing to start, and I reassured Ashley she would be OK and that I would talk to her later, after she woke up. She thanked me and added that she would like to talk to me privately when her boyfriend was not around. I nodded and said we would do that.

Ashley's request to talk to me without James around told me that my gut feeling regarding him and the conversation I'd had with them in ER, seemed to have a basis. I would have to wait and see what Ashley had to say. Her dilation and curettage was completed in just ten minutes, and by the end of the procedure, she had stopped bleeding completely. I helped the nurse and Dr. Murphy move Ashley from the operating table to her bed, thanked them both, and left. I first changed my scrubs and then went to the waiting room to talk to James.

I found him in front of the TV, watching the sports news. I pulled a chair up next to him and waited for a few moments, to see if he would stop watching TV to ask me anything about Ashley. He kept on looking straight at the TV. Eventually, without even looking at me, he said, "What's up, doc?"

"Would you like to know how Ashley is doing?"

"Yeah, sure. How is she?"

"She is just fine," I said.

He did not ask any questions. I decided not to volunteer any more information. As I stood up, I told him he could see her in about fifteen minutes in the recovery room, just across from the waiting room. When I started walking away, he said, "Oh, doc, when can she get pregnant again?"

I froze. It became immediately clear to me that theirs was an abusive relationship. I did not know if it were physically abusive, but it certainly looked like it was emotionally abusive. "Not for a while," I answered, and left the room, thinking to myself that I absolutely needed to talk to Ashley alone. This young woman needed help, both medically and emotionally. I decided to talk to social services the following morning to see if they might use the information I had to investigate further.

The following morning, I made it a point to go and see Ashley early in the morning, hoping that James would not yet be around. When I walked into her room, sure enough, she was alone. "You are doing quite well," I told her. "I plan to discharge you later in the day."
Ashley started crying. "Doc, I do not want to get pregnant again," she said. "He wants a baby at all costs, but I keep losing them. After the last one, I told him that before I got pregnant again I had to find out what was wrong. I had the money to pay a specialist. He was furious over why I wanted to spend all that money, and he went on a rampage at home. He found the money in the closet, took it away from me, and left the house." She paused for a moment. "I am afraid I am going to die trying to have a baby." She sobbed uncontrollably.
"Have you been physically abused?" I asked her. "No, but he drives me crazy. I think that, one of these days, that may happen too."

She told me she never used any birth control because he did not want to use condoms. I asked her if she knew anything about an IUD, or intrauterine device, which I could put into her uterus to prevent pregnancy.
"He does not have to know if you don't tell him," I told her. "Or I could prescribe some birth control pills."
"He is going to find out about the pill. When can I have the IUD in?" She asked.
"I can do it before you leave the hospital," I said. I also told her I was going to postpone her discharge until the following day. I still wanted to have social services come and talk to her, to see what they could do.

Ashley agreed and I asked her when James was going to come to see her.

"He won't come until I leave the hospital," she said.

"Then tell James we will discharge you tomorrow afternoon." That would give us time for social services to see her and for me to insert an IUD the following morning. I asked her whether there was anything else I could do for her. She thanked me for my help, but did not think I could do anything else.

Later that morning, I visited the head of the social services in the hospital. Helen was an experienced professional and I had worked with her before with other patients. She greeted me cordially, as usual, and told me, "I was expecting you. I heard about a young woman with seven lost pregnancies. Is that what you want to see me about?"

I smiled. "Who's the gossiper?"

"I have my sources," Helen said.

I proceeded to tell her Ashley's story. "There is no doubt in my mind that this young lady is in an abusive relationship—maybe not physical, if she is telling the truth, but certainly emotionally abusive. I can't believe he is subjecting her to miscarriage after miscarriage without any attempt at finding out what is going on."

Helen agreed and promised me she would personally take the case. She asked me to write an order for the nurse to bring Ashley to her office, where she would prefer to talk to her in privacy, rather than in Ashley's room, where her boyfriend may arrive unannounced. I thanked her, picked up the phone right there and dialed the nurse assigned to Ashley. I asked her to please bring Ashley to Helen's office.

"Thank you, Doctor Aladjem. I will do so. I am so glad," she replied. I thanked her and hung up. I looked at Helen and smiled again. "I know who the gossiper is."

"Go and finish your rounds," she said. "You are late."

I thought to myself what a pleasure it was to work with people who cared.

The following morning, as promised, I inserted an IUD into Ashley's uterus. She wouldn't get pregnant; she was protected for the time being. Helen called to give me a follow-up on Ashley. "It's worse than you think," she told me. "Come and see me."

Before the day was over, I returned to Helen's office. She proceeded to tell me that Ashley's abusive relationship was physical as well as emotional.
"I guess she did not want to tell you he abuses her physically as well. It's not unusual for patients to conceal that aspect," Helen added.

Two years ago, James had broken Ashley's wrist. Helen had the ER record. Ashley told them she had fallen, but the ER record indicated one does not get that type of lesion from falling. Helen continued to tell me that theirs had been an eight-year nightmare relationship, and that Ashley felt she could not get out of it. They did not live together, despite having been together for so long. Ashley had given Helen permission to approach the court and Helen was planning to ask the judge to issue a restraining order, so that Ashley could leave James.
"I'll see what else I can do for her," Helen said.

I felt sorry for Ashley. That afternoon I discharged her from the hospital but asked her to come and see me in four weeks for a follow-up. She agreed to come. I wished her well.

A month later, Ashley came to see me. She was a different person. She was neatly dressed, her hair was kept in place by a colorful sweatband, and she was smiling. "I want to thank you for everything you did for me," she said. "The social services lady got a restraining order for James," she continued. "I have not seen him since. He apparently had a history that I did not know about. The judge threatened to put him in jail and throw the key away if he dared to come near me. I am a human being again. Thank you."
It was such good news. I was delighted for her.
"I have a job in a store as a salesperson, and as soon as I have some money, I would like to come and see you and find out what's wrong with me."
I told Ashley she would have to see a fertility specialist, which I was not, although I would recommend one when she was ready.

But I would be happy to one day take care of her pregnancy, if and when she decided to get pregnant.

"Well, I will have first have to find a good man," she said, smiling. Ashley was happy, and her IUD was in place and gave her no trouble. I told to come and see me again in six months, and yearly thereafter, to ensure her IUD did not cause any problems. "OK," she agreed. "I will."

What do you mean it's more than one?

Multiple pregnancies (more than one baby in a single pregnancy) are common in certain animals, but are the exception in humans. The most common form of multiple pregnancies are twins. From 1915 to 1970 in the United States, the rate of twins was stable at about 2% of all births. After 1980, as a result of reproductive technologies used in the treatment of female infertility, the rate of multiple pregnancies increased to the point of being called "an epidemic of multiple pregnancies." Spontaneous occurrence of higher order multiples—such as triplets, quads, quintuplets, or more—are quite rare. In 2006, the rate of multiple pregnancies other than twins was 1.4 per 1000 births. Since that time, the trend appears to be decreasing. In spontaneously occurring multiple pregnancies, genetics seems to play a role, since most multiple pregnancies occur within the same families.

Unfortunately, as the number of babies in any single pregnancy increases, so do potential complications. Patients with multiple pregnancies are more likely to develop high blood pressure, have premature babies, and experience a multitude of other problems.

Sarah was in her second pregnancy when she first came to our office. Two years prior, her first child had been delivered somewhere on the west coast. Her husband, an engineer working for a major company, had been transferred to our area to head a subsidiary of the company. Sarah had experienced some problems during her first pregnancy and her physician had advised her to seek care with a maternal fetal medicine specialist in future pregnancies.

She was a teacher, but she was not planning to work while pregnant or for some time after delivery. Having two young children would keep her busy enough.

A pleasant young lady of twenty-six years of age, Sarah's last pregnancy had been complicated by gestational diabetes—a form of diabetes that manifests during pregnancy. She had been able to control her blood sugar with diet alone, so it was only during the last two months of pregnancy that she had needed to add insulin to her diabetic management. Her blood sugars returned to normal after the pregnancy was over. Currently, her blood sugar levels, which she had started checking once she realized she was pregnant, were fine. I suggested we perform an ultrasound and I would complete my examination afterward.

When I entered the ultrasound room, Sarah was already lying on the examining table. Based on her menstrual dates, I expected the pregnancy to be about sixteen weeks. But I noticed that her abdomen appeared enlarged over and beyond what I would have expected at that time in her pregnancy. My first thought was that her dates might have been wrong.

I began her ultrasound by passing over the entire abdomen, which gives me a first impression of what I am going to see or what to look for. To my surprise, it was immediately apparent this was not a single pregnancy, which explained why her abdomen seemed too large for her estimated twelve weeks of pregnancy.

I did not say anything to her just yet; I had to perform a detailed ultrasonographic examination. Slowly, I focused on the first infant, on her right. The fetus appeared normal, and so did the amniotic fluid. I then proceeded to the adjacent baby. Same finding. High in the upper part of the uterus, there was a third baby. This one appeared to have some problems. It was much smaller than the other two, and there was hardly any fluid. That was not good. I kept on scanning and, to my surprise, found a fourth infant. This one was lying down in the uterus, above the cervix, and appeared in good shape, just like the first two.

It took me some time to complete my first evaluation of the babies. Sarah, having had prior ultrasounds, was beginning to be suspicious. "Is there anything wrong with the baby," she asked. "Yes and no," I replied. "You have more than one baby. Let me show you."

Her face suddenly flushed. "What do you mean I have more than one? I really have twins?"
I paused for a moment. "Let's take a look."

I repositioned the ultrasound screen so she could see it. Then I brought into the screen the first two, which were positioned, respectively, to her left and right. I pointed to the first of the babies and showed her its heart beating normally and the amniotic fluid the baby was floating in. I then focused on the second one, and repeated the same view.
"Oh my," she whispered. "Twins. Oh my God."
"We are not finished yet," I told her. Moving the transducer, I showed her the third one, in the lower part of the uterus.
"Another one? I can't believe it."
"This one is normal as well," I reassured her. "We are not done yet, Sarah. There is a fourth, but this one has some problems." I directed the ultrasonic beam towards the upper part of her uterus, and the fourth baby made its appearance on the screen.
"What's the problem?" she asked with a tremor in her voice.

Compared with the other three, the fourth baby was moving in slow motion. I pointed out the limited amount of fluid surrounding the infant, barely enough for it to extend an extremity. It was also much smaller than the others. Tears welled in Sarah' eyes.
I suggested she get dressed and come into my office. "We need to talk."

I was sure Sarah was in shock. Who wouldn't be? It was clear to me that the fourth baby was unlikely to survive the pregnancy. The limited amount of fluid, also known as oligohydramnios, so early in pregnancy, was an ominous sign. The cause was unknown. Perhaps the sac of the fourth baby had broken early, emptying whatever fluid it had. There are other causes for such a limited amount of fluid, most of them with very a poor prognosis. To expect the infant to develop without any fluid that early in pregnancy was a long shot. Regardless, the cause, which we may or may not discover, would not change the very, very poor prognosis for this baby.

Renee, the nurse, brought Sarah into my office. She was a little shaky, and she had obviously been crying. I asked her to sit down and offered to have someone bring her coffee, tea or something cold. Sarah thanked me, but declined.

"I am sure you have a lot of questions," I told her. "But let me first give you some idea of where we go from here. Spontaneously having quads, without the intervention of reproductive technology, is very rare. Probably in the range of 1 in 700,000 births." I asked if she or her husband had a family history of multiple pregnancies. Indeed, there were twins in her family. Her sister had twins, and she believed her great-grandmother had twins also. She did not remember anyone else. In her husband's family, there was no history of twins or multiple births.

"Multiple pregnancies sometime run in families," I told her.

I reviewed what the ultrasound had showed and shared again my concern about the fourth baby, which I told her was unlikely to survive to the end of the pregnancy.

"What if the baby dies before delivery? How will it affect the other three?" Sarah asked.

I told her I believed the fourth baby would expire in a matter of days or weeks at most. Nothing needed to be done. Since she was so early in her pregnancy, the baby would just remain in the uterus without endangering the other three. Under the circumstances, this was nature's way of taking care of it. If it were later in pregnancy, the death of the baby could, theoretically, start labor and result in three premature infants, a situation that would not be at all desirable.

We also explored the potential problems associated with triplets. For the time being, Sarah could continue her usual life, without excesses. No running several miles a day, no bicycling, a controlled diet, no long trips anywhere unless I okayed it, and no sexual activity until further notice. "As time goes by," I told her, "I fully expect you may have to be hospitalized if premature labor threatens."

"I still can't believe all of this. Oh, my God. I can't wait to see Danny's face when I tell him the news," she said. "Would it be possible for my husband to see an ultrasound?"

"I will be happy to show him when he comes with you," I reassured her. "There are going to be a lot of ultrasounds in the future for you."

For some time, we continued to talk about what to expect and I answered her many questions. Last but not least, I performed my examination. When we were all done, I told her I would like to see her in two weeks time. If she had any problems in the meantime, she was to report them to me without delay. She also had to report her blood sugar levels twice a week.

At her next visit, Sarah was accompanied by Danny, her husband. He was a pleasant gentleman in his thirties.
"I thought Sarah was trying to kid me, when she first told me about this pregnancy. That's more than we bargained for," he said smiling. "We'll be busy, I guess."
"Indeed so," I replied.

Danny had a few questions and once I answered them, I proceeded to perform an ultrasound, not only to assess the progress of the pregnancy but primarily to see how the fourth baby was doing. It was no surprise to me to discover that the fourth baby had expired sometime after I first saw Sarah.

Receiving news of the death of a baby inside its mother's uterus, regardless of circumstances, is always traumatic experience for both parents. I showed both of them the three babies that were doing well. I could clearly see the sex of two of the babies—boys—but the third one was showing me the back, and I could not tell. I told them that, and Danny joked, "It has to be a girl. Women are always so temperamental."

"I am afraid I do not have very good news about the fourth one," I said.
Before I could continue, Sarah instantly said, "The baby is dead, is that true?"
"I am very sorry. You are right," I said.
She started crying softly and extended her hand to her husband, who took it and gave her a kiss. I stopped performing the

ultrasound, excused myself and stepped out of the room, realizing they needed to be alone for a while.

When I returned, Danny was still holding Sarah's hand. "I am very sorry about the fourth baby. There is nothing we could have done to change the natural course of events."
"We understand," replied Danny. "Let us now concentrate on the remaining three."

After the ultrasound, I suggested they both join me in my office to discuss our plans for the future. On leaving the room and I heard the nurse telling me that another patient was ready to see me. I asked her to show Danny and Sarah into my office whenever they were ready.

When I entered my office, they were both there waiting for me. Sarah still had an occasional tear, but she seemed composed. Danny wanted to know if there was anything that they would have to do right now, and I explained to him that nothing needed to be done at that time. Sometimes, retained dead babies may affect the ability of the mother's blood to clot normally. I did not think that was going to be the case with Sarah. "We will have to do some blood tests to monitor that possibility," I said.

Sarah was now almost eighteen weeks and her pregnancy was progressing nicely. She was showing, the increase in her abdomen very consistent with a multiple pregnancy. She had no bleeding or other problems. I was as optimistic as I could be. Her gestational diabetes was under excellent control, and diet appeared to suffice for managing it for the time being. If we were to have any problems, the most likely was going to be threatened premature labor, which is common in multiple pregnancies when compared to the slower growth of singletons, because the rapid increase in uterus size stimulates uterine contractions. Some women are more sensitive to these potential complications than others. Threatened premature labor usually first appears between twenty and twenty-four weeks, so I advised both of them that should Sarah feel any contractions, I needed to know without delay.

Sarah's pregnancy continued without major problems. Follow-up ultrasounds showed the growth of the three babies was normal. The infants were active, and the amount of fluid was unremarkable in all of them. Other fetal well-being tests also reassured us there were no apparent problems. At one of the visits, we determined that the third baby was indeed a girl. Sarah was elated. Danny had the look of "I told you so." At around twenty-three weeks or so, Danny had to go back to the west coast for a business meeting, and Sarah wanted to know if she could also travel. We were approaching a sensitive time in her pregnancy, the twenty-fourth week, and I did not think traveling would be wise. Although disappointed, Sarah agreed to stay home.

A few days later, at around eleven o'clock at night, I received a call from the emergency room doctor telling me Sarah had just been brought in by ambulance. She was contracting. I asked the ER doctor to admit her directly to the labor and delivery area, and called the labor and delivery nurse to alert her that Sarah would be coming and to instruct her to start intravenous fluids as soon as Sarah was admitted.

I arrived soon thereafter. The nurses had started the intravenous fluids I ordered and Sarah told me she had no bleeding and no leakage, a good sign. I asked the nurse to bring the portable ultrasound, as I wanted to see the babies and take a look at the cervix, to see if it showed any dilation. I could have performed a pelvic exam, but decided against it. Vaginal exams may predispose to vaginal infection, which would only enhance the contractions and may cause the membranes to rupture.

The ultrasound scan showed the infants were not lying on the cervix, and the cervix appeared closed and of good length—extremely good news, which I shared with Sarah. I decided to start intravenous medication to slow, and hopefully stop, contractions. The plan of action was explained to Sarah and I also told her that, for the time being, she would be on bed rest. She asked me how long she might be in the hospital. Unfortunately, I could not give her an answer at that time. Truly, I would not have been surprised

51

if she had to remain hospital for the duration of her pregnancy. Sarah told me that she had left her first child with a neighbor and good friend for the night, but that she would have to make some arrangements. I suggested it would be prudent to make arrangements for a long-term hospitalization.

Since I did not know whether my efforts to slow down labor would be successful, I decided to remain in the hospital that night, just in case labor ensued. I told Sarah I would be available all night.

The following morning, things were quiet. The medication had worked beautifully, and we could register only an occasional contraction, some of which Sarah did not perceive since they were very mild. But the uterus was not quiet. It was what we call an "irritable uterus." Experience told me I could not discontinue the medication, at least not for the time being. For the next few days, Sarah would continue to remain in the labor and delivery area and we would have to continue with her treatment.

Sarah understood and had no reservations about what we were doing. She had no questions either. She told me Danny was flying home that afternoon. On leaving the area, I asked the nurse assigned to Sarah's care to keep me posted about Sarah's condition on an hourly basis.

Things continued without any major changes. Contractions continued at a low level of intensity, and then began to space out. That was good news. The following morning, things were looking good. Sarah had hardly any contractions, so I decided to swap her intravenous medication for an oral one and transferred her from labor and delivery to the obstetrical unit.

The night that followed was quiet, and the following morning, Sarah was in good spirits. Danny returned home and was there early in the morning. I was pleased with Sarah's progress and told both of them that if everything continued to be stable, I might be able to discharge her the following morning. I also told Sarah to begin to walk around the obstetrical unit, not more than ten to fifteen minutes at a time. Danny asked me about the chances of the pregnancy continuing to term. I told him that such a possibility was unrealistic. "If we reach thirty-four weeks, we will be very happy," I said.

The following morning, things were still looking good. I decided to release Sarah from the hospital and instructed her to continue her bed rest or, if she preferred, to sit in a La-Z-boy chair. Her activities should be kept to a minimum. Essentially, she would be confined to her home and her oral medications would continues. I also instructed her in how to monitor her contractions herself, should they recur. I asked her to see me in a week and call the office with progress reports twice weekly, or at any time if needed.

The next week was quiet and Sarah came to her scheduled appointment. She had no complaints, except that her size made getting around difficult. I performed an ultrasound, and while the babies appeared to be doing well, I was not happy to see that her cervix had changed significantly. It had thinned out and shortened. It was, however, still closed. The change in shape meant that contractions were still occurring, even if Sarah did not feel them due to their low intensity. However, apparently the contractions were strong enough for the cervix to change, a sign that full-blown premature labor may not be far away. There was no question that Sarah had to be kept under surveillance in the hospital and receive intravenous medication. We were still a long way from our thirty-four weeks goal. Her pregnancy was barely twenty-five weeks along.

I shared my findings with Sarah and Danny, and told them I wanted to hospitalize Sarah. I explained why, and that by her being in the hospital, we hoped to be able to control any potential problems. Neither Sarah nor Danny objected. I also told them that, in all probability, she would remain in the hospital until her delivery time.

We admitted Sarah directly from my office to the obstetrical unit. I told her she would need bed rest until further notice and that I would see her shortly in the hospital. In the meantime, I called the labor and delivery nurse and gave her the initial orders, which included intravenous fluids and medication to completely calm

53

whatever uterine contractions Sarah may have had. The report of her nurse later that afternoon indicated that all was quiet and the ordered medication had been started. Once my office hours were done, I went directly to the obstetrical unit to check on Sarah.

She seemed to be comfortable. The monitor showed some uterine activity, so I put my hand on her abdomen and noted that the contractions, when they occurred, where of very low intensity since my fingers could easily indent the uterus during the contraction. That would not be possible during a strong contraction. I thought that the uterus would continue to be irritable and would probably remain like that. The question was: for how long?

When a patient is admitted to the obstetrical unit for what is expected to be a long stay, the nursing staff instinctively tries to make that stay homey. There are no special orders or protocols, or anything else. It just happens. Nurses who are not assigned to the patient will stop by to say hello or to ask if the patient needs anything special. They encourage the husband or the family to bring the woman's other children to the hospital to visit their mom, and they will prepare a cot or a La-Z-boy armchair for the husband or family member if they wish to stay overnight. The morning routine includes a stop by the patient's room to say hello, or to check that they had a good night.

It was no different in Sarah's case. Before you knew it, everyone knew Sarah well and everybody was rooting for her triplets. Sarah's personality was such that she not only appreciated the attention but made good friends with everybody. Some mornings, Danny would even bring in two dozen donuts for our morning coffee.

As we approached thirty weeks, Sarah started to have some difficulty breathing because of the size of her uterus. We told her to lie on her side, a more comfortable position for a pregnant woman than lying on her back. The people from occupational therapy were doing their part in keeping Sarah interested and occupied. Lifting the spirits of a patient during a prolonged hospitalization is of paramount importance.

We had some close calls when, suddenly and without warning, Sarah's uterus started contracting. Prompt intervention, fortunately, stopped the havoc and the uterus quieted down again. In the meantime, we introduced her to the neonatologists who would be called upon to take care of her triplets. We also suggested that Sarah and Danny visit the neonatal intensive care unit and familiarize themselves with that environment, where, most likely, their triplets would spend some time after birth.

The babies were doing surprisingly well. We estimated that should we reach thirty-four weeks, at the rate they were growing they would be born at close to five or six pounds each. Sarah's gestational diabetes was not giving us any trouble, and surprisingly, her diet alone was keeping her blood sugar within acceptable limits.

I was pleased with her progress. In fact, I was beginning to be more optimistic about perhaps reaching thirty-five or thirty-six weeks. I should have known better. The day she reached thirty-four weeks, her uterus started contracting, this time for real. I got a page from the nurse in charge telling me that Sarah was in "good labor." It was about eight o'clock in the morning and I was already in the hospital.

I went immediately to the obstetrical floor, but they had already moved Sarah to the labor and delivery area, a floor above. I rushed up the stairs. When I arrived, the clerk said, "She's in room five." The head nurse told me they had already alerted the neonatal team, and the operating room was ready in case I needed to do a cesarean section.

A simple look at Sarah told me that this was the day. I got a glove and proceeded to examine her. I also asked for the ultrasound equipment to be brought in.

During her stay in the hospital, we had talked several times about delivery and the likelihood that she would end up having a cesarean section. We talked about alternatives and how certain decisions would have to be made when the time came. Sarah told me that unless surgery became necessary, she wanted to have a natural childbirth, which was what she had with her first child. As I entered the room, Sarah asked me if I planned to do a cesarean section. I told her I would make that decision as soon as I finished examining her.

Multiple pregnancies usually end up delivering by cesarean section; however, if babies are positioned such that a vaginal delivery can be safely achieved, a cesarean section is not necessary.

Upon examining her, I felt the head of the first triplet coming down and felt that the cervix was almost completely open. I pulled the ultrasound equipment closer to the bed and quickly looked for the second triplet, which I found behind the first, also head down. The problem was the third baby, which was lying sideways in the upper portion of the uterus; that could be a problem. However, with the first two being head down and therefore expected to deliver uneventfully, I was confident I could handle the last one after the delivery of the first two. There was a good chance that after the delivery of the second baby, the third one would turn around, either head first or buttocks first. If it remained horizontal in the uterus, I would not be able to safely change its position. If that were the case, I would have to do a cesarean section. I explained all of this to Sarah, whose response was, "I trust you."

During all this time, three neonatologists and six nurses arrived at the door of Sarah's room. Each neonatologist formed a team with two nurses, and members of each team had an assigned number—1, 2 or 3—pinned on their backs. The numbers indicated whether they would take care of the first, second or third triplet. I told the nursing staff we would proceed with a vaginal delivery in the operating room and briefly informed everybody what to expect. There should not be a problem with the first two, and we should be ready for a cesarean section for the third, should I not feel that the baby could be safely delivered vaginally.

The three neonatologists went to the surgical room and began their preparations for a triplet delivery. The anesthesiologist was called and Sarah was moved into the operating room. I asked the head nurse to call Danny and let him know we are ready to deliver. I also asked her to accompany him into the Operating room, when he arrived. After making him don a gown, mask and shoe covers.

As chaotic as all this sounded, these were not the first triplets to be delivered in the hospital and everyone knew exactly what their role was. I scrubbed and went into the operating room. Sarah was on the table and the attached monitor showed the three heartbeats without any abnormalities. The anesthesiologist had placed an oxygen mask on Sarah, assuring proper maternal oxygenation, which is beneficial to the babies.

Upon examining Sarah again, I found the head of the first baby down and almost ready to be delivered. This was a good time to break its membranes, since they were still intact. A gush of clear fluid rushed down. That was good, since clear fluid indicates the baby is doing well. I asked Sarah to bear down with her next contraction. Slowly, the perineum stretched, the head rotated from the left side of the mother to the middle and, without much delay, stretched the perineum even more until the baby's head literally popped out into my waiting hands. I gently maneuvered the rest of the body out, and clamped and cut the cord. It was a boy. I handed him to the neonatology first nurse. She took him and placed him in a warm incubator and the neonatologist took over. The baby cried almost immediately thereafter.

At about that time, Danny walked into the operating room. "Did I miss anything?" he asked.
"The first one is a boy. Congratulations."
He went to peek at the baby and then moved directly to Sarah and held her hand.

Following the delivery of the first triplet, things quieted down for about ten minutes or so. "I feel like pushing again," Sarah said. "Take it easy," I replied. "Let me see where we are." I could feel the head of the second triplet through the intact membranes. It was on its way down. The uterus continued to contract well, judging by Sarah's moans.
"Can I push?" Sarah asked.

"Yes. Gently, not too hard."
She did so and the head slowly came down, allowing me to break
the membranes of the second triplet. A gush of clear fluid followed.
"Next contraction, give me a good push," I instructed. She did. In
one push, the baby's head appeared on the thinned perineum and,
without any effort, the second triplet delivered. It was the second
boy.

After cutting the cord, I handed the baby to the number two
neonatology nurse. This baby, too, cried instantly. The second
neonatologist took over and began examining the baby.

The delivery of the second triplet was followed by a period of
calm. I asked for the ultrasound equipment to be brought in next
to Sarah, took my gloves off, and started to scan, looking for the
position of the third baby. It was still in the upper uterus, with its
bag of water intact. Should the membranes break while the baby
was still horizontal across the uterus, it would become difficult, if
not impossible, to attempt to change its position because the uterus
will clamp down on the baby's body. Gloving myself again, I made
the decision to wait awhile and see what, if anything, happened
without my intervention.

Sure enough, upon examining Sarah, I found that the baby's
buttocks were slowly beginning to come down. I warned
everybody we would have a breech delivery for the third triplet and
told Sarah to push only when I asked her to, and to breathe when
she felt contractions. "Everything's OK," I reassured her.

With each contraction, Sarah was breathing as instructed. I could
feel the breech coming down and the membranes remained intact. I
was also able to establish that it was what we call a "frank breech,"
in which the lower extremities are flexed at the hips and extended
at the knees. The membranes continued to remain intact and,
slowly but surely, the breech was coming down towards the lower
part of the pelvis.

The contractions were steady and strong, so I told Sarah to
start pushing. With the baby's buttocks well into the pelvis, the

membranes broke spontaneously. I checked her immediately
to make sure the umbilical cord was not trapped between the
maternal bones and the baby; this was not the case, and the baby's
heart monitoring was strong and reassuring.

I continued to ask Sarah to push with each contraction, which
brought down the baby and spontaneously delivered the lower part
of the body. It was time to intervene. Gently, I first delivered one
leg, then the other. With the legs freed from the pelvis, I took a
towel from the instrument table and wrapped the baby's lower body
in it, which served two purposes: to protect the infant's abdomen
from the pressure of my hands, and to make the baby less slippery.
Rotating the body first towards one side of the mother and then to
the other, I easily delivered the arms, one at a time. Finally, lifting
the baby's body upward allowed for the head to descend and deliver
it without difficulty. I cut and clamped the cord and handed the last
of the triplets to the third neonatology nurse.

There must have been some tension in the room, because as
soon as the third baby cried, everybody applauded. "You were
wonderful," I told Sarah. "Congratulations."
"Thank you for your help," she said.
All that remained to be done was to deliver the placentas. Sarah
was comfortable and in no pain. I checked her perineum and
birth canal and found them to be intact without tears. As I was
examining her, a gush of blood issued from the uterus—a sign
one of the placentas was beginning to separate from the uterus.
I pulled gently on each of the three cords to see which one had
loosened. The first and the second cord were loosening and another
gush of blood came from the vagina. Following it were the two
placentas, which I removed without any problem. They looked to
be intact, which is important to note, since any remnants inside the
uterus may cause postpartum bleeding. One placenta remained, in
addition to the sac of the dead fourth triplet.

I thought the sac of the fourth baby was going to come together
with the remaining placenta. We waited for almost ten minutes,
and then a tug on the remaining cord was followed by a gush

of red blood, suggesting the remaining placenta was on its way. Slowly, I tugged gently until the final placenta—the largest of the three—came down and was removed. After removing it, I pressed upon the uterus to ensure it was contracting well, and then I took the entire removed tissue and placed it on my instrument table. Sure enough, there was an amorphous mass in addition to the placenta of the third twin. It was the dried sac of the fourth baby. Opening it, I indeed found the fourth fetus, or I should say, what once was a fetus but was now what we call a Papyraceus Fetus—a dried out, paper thin fetus with only the contour of a fetus—the result of reabsorption of the dead fetus. The fourth fetus may have died because of poor implantation of its placenta, which was unable to support the baby, or some other problem that is not always apparent. In such cases, we always send the material to the pathologist for microscopic diagnosis, hoping they may have an answer as to why the baby died.

Both Sarah and Danny wanted to know what had happened to the fourth fetus. I told them that the sac was delivered, and Danny wanted to see it while Sarah did not. I accompanied Danny to the instrument table and explained to him what he was looking at. He thanked me and returned to Sarah's side.

By then, the triplets were clean and dressed. They weighed, respectively, six pounds, five pound eight ounces, and five pound six ounces. The neonatologists assured me they were all OK, breathing without problems, and would remain under observation in the neonatal intensive care unit for now.

Sarah had an uneventful postpartum course, so we made plans for discharge as soon as she felt up to going home. When Sarah and her triplets went home, the mood on the obstetrical unit and the post-partum unit was festive. Sarah and Danny promised they would all visit once things normalized.

I saw Sarah and Danny when she came for her six weeks postpartum visit. The triplets came too. Needless to say, everyone in the office was delighted to see them. Danny brought a big cake as a thank you. I asked him how life was going with triplets at home.

"Well, days are OK. Nights are a little rough. They have to be fed around two o'clock in the morning. Sarah and I take turns. Sometimes, I'm not sure if I've fed one of them three times or if I've fed the three of them once."
Everyone had a good laugh.

* * *

A little blood is scary

Blood has always been looked upon with awe and reverence. Its significance to survival well rooted in history and tradition. Throughout centuries, popular superstitions related to blood have run rampant, from vampires, to isolating women who were menstruating, to bloodletting and to the lunar effect on clotting, which precluded physicians from operating during certain lunar phases. In the absence of science, superstitions prevailed.

Hippocrates, circa 400 years BC, believed blood was one of the four humors, together with phlegm, yellow bile and black bile. This belief was at the core of the medicine practiced by Greek, Roman, Islamic, and eventually European, physicians until the nineteenth century. Hippocrates' theory held that health was the result of a balance between these four humors. Any disease was due to their imbalance.

In the Judeo-Christian tradition, blood is "the life of the flesh" (Leviticus 17:11). A differentiation was always made between the life-giving blood seen in childbirth and the blood of injury and/or death. Misconceptions about blood and circulation were perpetuated by physicians of the time. In a woman of reproductive age, the lack of menstrual period associated with pregnancy, has been observed and established since early times. Bleeding while pregnant was always considered a scary occurrence, since it indicated an abnormal pregnancy, and often preceded the loss of that pregnancy; this is as true today as it was thousands of years ago.

When Sophia came to see me, she was about five weeks pregnant, based on her last menstrual period. She had been married for some six years, and both she and her husband wanted to start a family. They were both in their mid-thirties, both goal- and career-oriented individuals. Unfortunately, her three previous attempts to have children had failed due to miscarriages, for no apparent reason. She was now pregnant for the fourth time. Needless to say, Sophia was a nervous wreck, and her husband was not any better.

Sophia had no problem getting pregnant, but all of her pregnancies were complicated by early bleeding, and her three miscarriages occurred in a similar fashion. She was told to take bed rest and given hormonal shots to "support the pregnancy," but inevitably, by the end of the second month or beginning of the third month, the bleeding became excessive and she miscarried shortly thereafter. Having missed a period, her physician confirmed that Sophia was pregnant again and she was referred to my office.

To my surprise, she, too, had never evaluated the possible cause of her repeated miscarriages. While it is true that in most early miscarriages no real cause can be identified, it is also true that in cases where a cause can be identified, something can often be done to prevent further miscarriage. I explained this to Sophia and her husband, and I especially asked why nothing had been done to seek a cause following her second miscarriage. Sophia told me her doctor had offered some evaluations, but she had declined since she wanted to get pregnant again as soon as possible.

I have seen this happen over and over again. Some women delay pregnancy until their career is established, and by that time, they feel time is running out and rush into a pregnancy fully expecting they will have no problems. Some don't have any issues; but some do, and those who do, find themselves into a quandary—just like Sophia. Not only do they become fearful that time is running out but, subconsciously, their desperate desire to prove they can have a routine pregnancy, like everybody else, pushes them to deny the possibility that something may be wrong. Consequently, they keep trying for a new, healthy pregnancy, but when that does not happen, the psychological trauma can be significant.

During our conversation, something Sophia's husband had said caught my attention. At one point, he expressed the thought: "If she cannot carry a pregnancy, we might as well give up."
I felt that, psychologically, they were on the dangerous road of finger-pointing and blaming, which is not unusual in such cases but can wreck a relationship and end a marriage.

I told them that before we went any further, I wanted to proceed with a detailed ultrasound to see where we were at. They agreed. I also explained to them that, because of the early gestation, we would have to proceed with a trans-vaginal ultrasound for better visualization, in addition to the traditional trans-abdominal view.

Sophia's husband opted to not be present during the ultrasound session, which was unusual and reinforced my thoughts that perhaps not all was well in that relationship. When we got to the ultrasound room, Sophia told me her husband was "very upset" with her for losing three pregnancies. I told her to keep in mind that it was not her fault.

The ultrasound confirmed her pregnancy at about six to seven weeks gestation. Her cervix, or the mouth of the uterus, was perfectly normal in length and was closed, as it should be. What I found, however, was that she had two small fibroids located on the back wall of the uterus and protruding slightly into the uterine cavity. Fibroids, or fibroid tumors, are a benign, non-cancerous growth of fibrous tissue, and are not uncommon. If located on the outside of the uterus, they rarely interfere with a pregnancy; but those that protrude within the cavity of the uterus may interfere with the pregnancy, particularly if the placenta happens to implant where the fibroid is located. The good news, in this case, was that the placenta was implanted on the opposite side of the uterus, away from the fibroids.

I shared my findings with Sophia and asked her if she wanted to rejoin her husband so we could all talk about what needed to be done. She did.

Sophia did not know she had fibroids. I would assume, by their size, that they had been there before, but I could not exclude the possibility that this was a new finding. I explained to them that if the fibroids had been there during the previous pregnancies, it was conceivable that the placenta may have implanted near the fibroids, which may have caused bleeding and, eventually, miscarriage. A review of her previous ultrasound scans would shed some light on this issue.

More importantly, I wanted to talk to both of them about the prospects for this pregnancy, in view of my findings. We discussed the possible multiple causes of early miscarriages due to fibroids. Because of the hormonal environment during pregnancy, fibroids may become bigger, so what may not appear to be a major problem to start with, may become one later on during pregnancy. "Spotting and bleeding may occur during this pregnancy," I told them, "and may originate from the sites of the two protruding fibroids. As long as it is not coming from the placenta, such bleeding should be manageable and not cause major difficulties."

As a precaution, however, decreased activity, at least until the pregnancy was well established, was desirable, and intercourse was off limits.

"Well," her husband interrupted. "How is she going to manage her work?"

"That is Sophia's and your decision." My advice was that consideration should be given to a leave of absence from work, or work from home if possible.

"I do a lot of travel for my work," said Sophia, "work that I cannot do from home."

I told them that I could only advise what I thought was prudent, based on my best judgment. It was their decision to make. It was apparent that her husband had become uncomfortable with our discussion. After some short exchanges between them, her husband finally said, "Do what you want, Sophia. You are going to lose it anyhow, and you know that."

I was stunned. I had no idea what their personal relationship was like at that point in time, and I understood that perhaps he was as frustrated as she was, but I never tolerated situations where the husband was playing a blame game. In the interaction between an obstetrician and a couple, there are circumstances when the physician must take a stand and set someone straight. I strongly felt this was one of those situations.

"How do you know that?" I asked. "I am the physician, and I do not know that for sure."

Taken by surprise, he retreated very rapidly. "No, I mean, we have been through this three times. What's the point?" he said, somewhat apologetically.

"That is a question you should have asked before you agreed to attempt a new pregnancy. She did not get pregnant by herself. The point is: Sophia is pregnant. It is both your child and hers, and the question is: do you want to do your best for this pregnancy or not, regardless of unknown outcome at this time? If not, abortion is legal in this country, you know." I got my point across. "I am sorry," he said. "I did not say it right."

"I will stop working," said Sophia, "and we'll hope for the best." After a moment, her husband took her hand, looked at her, and said, "I agree. We'll manage."

I was pleased. At least for the time being, it appeared we were back on track. We spent a fair amount of time talking about what they could expect, the concept that other factors might have contributed to her miscarriages, the risk of a repeat occurrence and, if that were to occur, what needed to be done before attempting another pregnancy.

Sophia's pregnancy continued uneventfully until around twenty-two weeks, when she had an episode of spotting, followed by some very minor bleeding. She came to my office in a panic. There was no apparent reason for the spotting and bleeding. The infant was doing well. An ultrasound showed no source of bleeding from the placenta—the most likely source of such an episode.

I calmed her down and tried to make some sense of it all. Her examination was normal, and there was no source of bleeding from the vagina or the cervix. Spotting during pregnancy is not that unusual, although we would rather not have it as it is always of concern to both patient and doctor.

I asked her to recall when and how she first noted the spotting, but she did not give any history that could have explained it. She claimed not to have had intercourse or any vaginal trauma. I was unable to come up with any rational explanation. A diagnosis of unknown etiology is not a diagnosis: it only tells us that we don't know.

I assured Sophia that she was doing well, and that, other than continuous observation for a repeat episode, I had nothing to offer. I asked her to call me immediately if it happened again.

Her pregnancy continued without any other bleeding episodes. Despite that, Sophia continued to have a high level of anxiety. I could certainly understand her concerns. With her history, a little bleeding could be very scary.

She eventually delivered a healthy baby about a week before her due date. The examination of the placenta showed it to be entirely normal and it did not give us an answer as to where the bleeding may have come from.

It had been a long pregnancy for Sophia, and for me.

* * *

SECTION 2:

ALONG THE WAY

Myths and facts of pregnancy

It is human nature to consider pregnancy a miracle. For many, existence alone is credited to some supernatural intervention and each religion has its own story to explain our existence on this planet. In Judeo-Christian religions, God created Adam, the first man, in his own image. Eve was then also created by divine intervention, constructed from one of Adam's ribs. It was only after the original sin that we started to procreate and multiply

From time immemorial, our fear of the unknown allowed superstitions to govern our lives and shape our beliefs. In the absence of science, superstitions, faith, and beliefs were our guides to influence what we wanted to happen, or what we wanted to avoid happening.

Pregnancies were the prime target of such superstitions. With the passage of time, many pregnancy superstition or "old wives' tales" became myths. Some, such as that cutting cloth in bed may result in the baby having a cleft lip and palate, are still believed today, well into the twenty-first century.

During my career, I have encountered such myths many times. The mothers who held stock in them were not uneducated or illiterate by any means. Even in our technological age, with instant information at our fingertips and medical advances never before possible, pregnancy is special. When confronted with the unknown, our deep-rooted feelings and fears surface.
"Just in case, I want to know..." is how most superstitious people frame questions about pregnancy myths.

I am not referring to so-called myths, which might actually have a medical basis, like "a pregnant woman should not travel by plane," or "pregnant women should not exercise." These are genuine medical questions that a pregnant woman may have and that require an answer.

I am talking about some of the more unusual myths I encountered from my patients. It is not my intent to make fun of those who asked me such questions. What fascinated me was how genuine, even for the most unusual one, these questions were. There was always a true concern behind the myth, however unlikely.

Pregnancy myths vary from culture to culture, most, however, are universal, which speaks to the commonality of pregnancy worldwide and its intrinsic mystery as a stage of life. How else would we explain, for example, that thousands of years ago, in antiquity, the Egyptians believed the soul of the baby was contained in the placenta? They revered it, embalmed it, and kept it throughout the life of the individual until his or her death, when the placenta was buried with that individual so that the soul would continue in the afterlife. In the Andes of Peru, on the other hand, it is believed that each pregnant woman carries two lives in her womb: that of the baby and that of the placenta. At the time of birth, because of the attention the newborn receives, the placenta may show signs of envy, and if not controlled, may hurt the baby. That is why, after birth, the infant's father takes the placenta out of the village and buries it deep in the ground, so that no one will find it or no animal will recover it. The liberation of the placenta would allow its soul to damage the newborn.

Two cultures, thousands of miles apart, considered the placenta to have a soul. In Ancient Egypt, it had to be preserved because it contained the soul of the individual. In Peru, it had to be buried because its soul may be vindictive.

In Colombia, if a newborn did not breathe and was cold at the time of birth, the remedy was to heat the placenta. In the Talmud, if a newborn is not breathing or is underweight, it is recommended that the placenta be spread over its body.

In western cultures, afterbirth is usually discarded. But even then, some individuals think the mother should eat the placenta to absorb the hormones and vitamins it contains. In essence, this belief is little different to old myths about the placenta and the pregnancy. In our times, we explain it with some science: it is good for you.

One patient I treated was of Eastern European descent. In her culture, if a cat crossed the path of a pregnant woman, the child would be born with a birthmark on its face, of the same color as the cat. Her mother, who had come from the old country, had told her that and instructed her that if a cat crossed her path she was to spit in the wind three times while placing her hand on her abdomen. I do not know if she ever had the opportunity to follow her mother's advice.

Morning sickness is common in pregnancy. Over the years, I heard many myths about this unpleasant condition. One of my patients was absolutely convinced she was carrying a girl because her morning sickness was so bad; she had a boy. Of course, it could have just as well been a girl, which would have reinforced her belief. In the introduction to this book, I mentioned the question a young lady with bad vomiting in early pregnancy had asked: whether I thought she could vomit her baby. I do not know whether that was a myth she heard somewhere or whether it was a question generated in desperation. It could have been either—or both. The other myth related to morning sickness is that it starves the baby. Unlikely.

In western society, it is common for mothers to throw baby showers, where friends and family come with gifts for the soon-to-be-born baby. In other cultures, however, buying things for an unborn baby, or preparing a room for an expected child before it is born, is a bad omen. This myth dates back hundreds of years and is a superstition that took root because of high infant mortality in the past. Thus, not preparing anything in advance for the child fooled the evil spirits who did not know a baby would be forthcoming.

Food has always been associated with a rich selection of pregnancy myths. You want a girl? Your diet should be rich in dairy products, nuts, and soy. You want a boy? Salty foods and plenty of meat will do it. You want your baby to have plenty of hair? Make sure you eat a lot of spicy foods. Here, I have to pause for a moment. I remember reading a study that actually looked at this issue. The study concluded that indeed the mothers of babies born with a lot of hair loved spicy foods! Among the more ominous foods, bananas have the worst reputation. Some believe that eating green bananas may cause a miscarriage and eating a twin banana may lead to the birth of Siamese twins. If you eat crabs, on the other hand, your child may be hyperactive. This one seems to me to be a new myth, rather than an old one.

Trying to determine the sex of an unborn baby can probably claim the most persistent myths. Food cravings, which are known to occur in early pregnancy and sometimes persist throughout pregnancy, have notoriously been used to predict the sex of a baby. For example, if you crave oranges, lemons or other citrus food, it's a girl. If you crave salty foods, it's a boy. Sugary foods, anyone? It's a girl. The only craving a pregnant woman should be concerned about is a sudden hankering for chalk, dirt, or paint chips! Such cravings are indicative of a disease called pica, and a pregnant woman suffering them should talk to a doctor immediately.

Other myths about the baby's sex are that if you sleep on the left side, it's a boy. On the right side, it's a girl. If your hands are dry, it's a boy. If your hands are soft, it's a girl. If you carry low, it's a boy. If you carry high, it's a girl. If you dream you have a boy, it's going to be a girl. If you dream you gave birth to a girl, it's a boy. To take the guesswork out of this equation, I suggest having an ultrasound.

Keeping pregnancy a secret for the first few months is still common in many parts of the world. Sometimes this is merely prudent, due to a higher rate of miscarriage in early pregnancy, but the fear that some evil eye may damage the pregnancy is still deeply rooted. Also common is the recommendation that a woman should never raise both arms above her head because the baby might entangle in its own umbilical cord and die. Some eastern cultures believe that a woman should never cross a river during her last two months of pregnancy. Others believe they must always carry a knife with them when they go out, to ward off evil spirits.

It is not always easy to understand where such myths come from. In some cases, such as keeping pregnancy a secret during the first few months, the explanation is simple: most miscarriages occur during the first two months. Furthermore, having a miscarriage in some cultures is a stigma for not being able to carry a pregnancy, so not telling anyone avoids that stigma should the woman suffer a miscarriage. Even not crossing a river during the last two months could be explained away by the fact that the woman is quite heavy, has little stability, and to a certain degree, is clumsy. Since crossing a river in some cultures means, most likely, getting into a small boat, one can see that it might be dangerous. Others are more difficult to explain, but most likely go back thousands of years, their origins long forgotten while the myths live on.

When all is said and done, myths relating to pregnancy all demonstrate concern for the future mother and her baby's well-being. Most have been passed from generation to generation by word of mouth. While a woman may hear such myths from strangers, more usually it is her mother or a close family member who will instruct her in such rituals. I remember patients telling me about myths that came from a stranger and invariably dismissing them as "silly." I rarely heard them so easily dispelled when the myth was told by a woman's mother or mother-in-law. Implicit in that belief was that the woman's mother or family member had only the mother and child's well-being at heart. A stranger might not be so concerned, or might actually be evil. When it comes to these things, little has changed over centuries of motherhood, and I do not think some of these things will ever change. The miracle of birth still keeps us all in awe, and still keeps us guessing to a certain extent.

An unusual headache

Charlotte was in her early forties and had been a patient of mine for her previous two pregnancies because she suffered from gestational diabetes, a type of diabetes that appears only during pregnancy. A family history of diabetes made Charlotte very self-conscious of the fact that she was at risk of developing diabetes even when she was not pregnant. As a result, she was careful not to gain weight over and above her expected gain, she spot-checked her blood sugar once or twice a week, she watched her diet, and she exercised three to four times a week. When she became pregnant again, Charlotte was in the best possible shape and she was now about eight weeks pregnant. As it turned out, her gestational diabetes was the least of our problems.

About two weeks after I saw her for the first time in this pregnancy, Charlotte called to tell me she was experiencing a lot of nausea and vomiting. It was reasonable to assume it was pregnancy related. She had no other complaints, so I asked her to keep in touch if it worsened and gave her some basic instructions, all common in such situations.

Ten days later, she called me again. In addition to the nausea and vomiting, which had not subsided, she also had a significant headaches, almost like migraine headaches. She could not tell whether her nausea was now due to her headaches. This was unusual, so I asked her to come and see me at her earliest convenience.

Charlotte came into my office the next morning. She did not look sick. Her symptoms, however, concerned me. Her vomiting was not typical of pregnancy and occurred suddenly and unexpectedly, like an explosion. In addition, Charlotte's headaches did not sound like migraine headaches at all. She had no history of headaches and they were not persistent like migraines, but came and went. They were also more severe in the morning, something not usually seen in migraines. Her examination was also unremarkable.

I shared my concerns with Charlotte, telling her that the symptoms seemed less and less to be pregnancy related. I thought they may be the result of increased pressure in her brain and told her I would like her to have a brain MRI (Magnetic Resonance Imaging) to rule out the possibility of a brain problem.

Charlotte asked me bluntly if I thought she had a brain tumor. I told her I could not tell, but we had to make sure it was not. A number of other potential issues may result in the brain-related symptoms Charlotte had. For example, certain vascular abnormalities that one is born with but that only begin to be symptomatic in adulthood. Such abnormalities are known as aneurysms, and are like the ballooning of an artery. Given enough pressure, one can burst with tragic consequences such as brain hemorrhage. If detected in time, most can be repaired.

I made the radiology appointment and talked to the radiologist about my concerns. Charlotte was seen the following day. Later that day, the radiologist called my office and told me Charlotte had a meningioma—a brain tumor arising from the membranes that surround the brain and spinal cord. It was a medium-size tumor, and based on its location, he thought it to be readily accessible to surgery, if necessary.

Charlotte came to see me the next day to find out the results of her MRI. I shared the findings. Her first question was, "Will I make it through the pregnancy?"
I told Charlotte the good news was that most meningioma tumors were benign and their growth was usually slow. However, I wanted her to see a neurosurgeon for evaluation.

As expected, Charlotte had quite a few questions. Most of them had to do with pregnancies associated with this type of tumor. How would the baby be affected, if at all? Was it hereditary? One would expect that having just been diagnosed with a brain tumor, Charlotte would be eager to find out more about her tumor and her own prospects, but this was not the case with Charlotte. Maternal instincts took over and Charlotte's main concern was the well-being of her baby. Such behavior is not the exception, but the rule.

I have seen it happen many times. Maternal instincts are so strong that a mother-to-be focuses entirely on her infant's survival. I referred Charlotte to a neurosurgeon. She declined any medication for her nausea or headaches, simply saying, "I'll manage."

The neurosurgeon was optimistic about her prognosis. He thought the tumor must have been developing silently for a while. He was concerned about her symptoms and about the possibility that other symptoms, such as seizures, could occur if the tumor applied further pressure on the brain. Furthermore, pregnancy could accelerate the tumor growth, potentially leading to other consequences. Unfortunately, there was no way to predict the possibility of seizures or whether pregnancy would accelerate the tumor's growth. From the MRI review, his opinion was that the tumor was accessible and that, given the circumstances, removing it should be considered. Charlotte was now facing brain surgery.

The following week, she and her husband, whom I knew from previously taking care of Charlotte, came to my office. Both had also met with the neurosurgeon. I asked her how she was feeling. She was still vomiting several times a day and her headaches were not improving.
"What do you really think is going to happen to me?" she asked.
I told her that from my conversation with the neurosurgeon, I was optimistic. Meningiomas are usually benign, but their growth can cause serious complications. I trusted the neurosurgeon's opinion that the best course of action at this time was to remove the tumor.
"I understand that," she said, "but give me the worst case scenario."
"The worst case scenario would be that the tumor is malignant,"
I said, but I doubted that to be true. My best judgment was that Charlotte would do well.
"If it is malignant, will I be able have this baby?" asked Charlotte.
I perfectly understood what she wanted to know. "I must tell you again that the vast majority of meningiomas are benign," I answered. "The MRI appearance is not that of a malignant tumor, even though we will not know for sure until we have it in the pathologist's hand. To directly answer your question, the answer is yes."

"That is good to know," Charlotte said. Charlotte went on to tell me that she needed to tell the girls about her health, and wanted to be realistic. She also wanted to plan her life accordingly. It was important to her to know how this might affect her pregnancy, if at all. She definitely did not want to jeopardize the infant with whatever treatment might be required. I assured her that the surgery would not affect the infant, and that if further treatment were needed, like radiation or chemotherapy, we would discuss it at that time. We had ways to protect the infant.

The following week, Charlotte underwent surgery. The neurosurgeon's optimism regarding her prognosis proved to be right: the tumor was benign and was completely removed without any problems.

When I visited Charlotte in the hospital, she was happy and looking forward to her pregnancy. "I am so glad we took care of this," she said. "I never thought my vomiting was something other than morning sickness. Thank you for your help."

Charlotte's pregnancy continued without any major problems. Her diabetes remained in controlled throughout the remainder of her pregnancy and she reached term and delivered a seven pound, three ounces healthy baby boy.

* * *

Will my baby be born early?

For a pregnancy to run a successful nine-month course, many factors must work in harmony. Most of these factors are known. One is that the cervix, also known as the mouth of the uterus, should remain tightly closed throughout the pregnancy until delivery. During pregnancy, the uterus contracts mildly, having a progressive effect upon the cervix. As a result, the cervix softens, particularly towards the end of the pregnancy. When labor starts, the uterine muscle must work upon the cervix for several hours in order to pull it upwards, which eventually results in the cervix opening and allowing the infant to be born. There are also hormonal and other factors that facilitate these changes. All of this must work in perfect synchronization to allow the pregnancy to end successfully.

For reasons that are mostly unknown, the cervix does not always function as expected. At times, it does not open during labor, a condition known as "cervical dystocia." Or it may open before term, resulting in premature delivery, or even very early in pregnancy, in which case a miscarriage may occur. The premature opening of the cervix in early pregnancy is known as an "incompetent cervix." We do not always know the cause, but when a cervix develops a tear in a prior pregnancy, or when some other trauma occurs to change the cervical structure, the cervix may become incompetent. If the incompetence is detected in time, one can intervene and place a suture around the partially open cervix, tying and closing it; such a procedure is known as a "cerclage."

Natalie was twenty-eight years old when she came to see us. She had experienced two prior miscarriages, at twelve and seventeen weeks respectively. The last one had occurred four years ago. After her earlier miscarriage, Natalie had started taking birth control pills, but four months earlier she had stopped the birth control and had become pregnant. She thought she was probably two to three months along.

When asked if she knew why she had miscarried twice before, Natalie had no answer. She was just told that she miscarried. A dilation and curettage, which is a scrapping of the uterus after a miscarriage to remove any tissue left behind, was performed after each of her miscarriages.

It is unfortunate that most women get pregnant after a miscarriage without making an attempt to determine the reason for the miscarriage, because steps may be taken to correct the problem so that another miscarriage does not occur.

Natalie's examination showed her to be a healthy young lady. An ultrasound established that her pregnancy was somewhere between thirteen and fourteen weeks gestation.

My concern was that the two D & C's Natalie had undergone may have traumatized her cervix. It was conceivable that the first dilation and curettage may have damaged the cervix, creating a tear. That would explain the second miscarriage, but not the first. However, her second pregnancy may have been lost because of an incompetent cervix. In addition, the D & C after the second loss may have further aggravated the cervical damage, which would increase her risk of a miscarriage this time.

An ultrasound of her cervix showed some irregularity in its shape, and reinforced my concern about a cervical trauma. Her cervix was, however, closed. I told Natalie we would perform an ultrasound every two weeks until I was satisfied she did not have an incompetent cervix. I explained what exactly that meant and what we might have to do to avoid her potentially losing this pregnancy.

Natalie understood my concern. I made an appointment for her to return in two weeks. In the meantime, I suggested she refrain from having intercourse, avoid strenuous exercise such as running, and report any abnormality.

Two weeks later, her ultrasound showed no changes. She was now sixteen weeks and apparently doing well. Her next ultrasound was rescheduled in another two weeks. About a week after her visit, however, Natalie called and reported some cramping, but no bleeding or leakage. I asked her to come into the office without delay.

The ultrasound that same afternoon showed definite changes in her cervix. It was shortening and it was not tightly closed. I discussed these changes and suggested we perform a cerclage. One has to be very cautious, since the cerclage, like any other surgical procedure, may have complications. Finding the balance between risk and benefits is not always easy. Natalie understood and decided she needed more time to think about whether to undergo surgery. She did not want to jeopardize her pregnancy. She asked how much of a window she had to make her decision. Unfortunately, I could not give her a straight answer. Changes in the cervix, in some cases, may take hours, days, or may stay as is for a long time. I suggested she make a decision as soon as possible. Because the cervix was no longer tightly closed, there was also a risk of infection, or that the membranes may rupture.

Two days later, Natalie called and said she had decided to risk the cerclage rather than potentially risk another miscarriage.

I admitted her to the hospital that very morning. We started intravenous medication to quell any uterine irritability, and late that afternoon, we went ahead and performed a cerclage. After surgery, an ultrasound confirmed the cervix was now tightly closed. We kept Natalie in the hospital overnight and the following morning her uterus showed no contractions, the infant was doing well, and Natalie was feeling fine.

Upon discharge, Natalie was given instructions as to what she could or could not do, and was asked to report any contractions, leakage or bleeding, immediately.

At her next visit, Natalie was still pleased, happy, and looking forward to the rest of her pregnancy. We continued to examine her cervix at regular intervals and the ultrasound showed there were no changes, which was promising.

By the time we reached twenty-four weeks, her uterus started having some contractions. Not enough to be painful, but enough to be felt. Upon her arrival, Natalie told me that she and her husband had engaged in intercourse the night before. Soon after, she had felt her abdomen tightening. I was not happy. I had warned her intercourse could start contractions.
"I was feeling so well," she explained, "that I did not think it mattered anymore."

I admitted Natalie to our high-risk unit and started monitoring her contractions. They did not appear to be terribly strong, but unless we stopped them without delay, I expected a full-blown premature labor. Intravenous medication to calm the uterus was started immediately. It took several hours for her contractions to subside completely. I kept Natalie in the hospital for another twenty-four hours. Oral medication to keep the uterus quiet was prescribed, and she was to take the medication every six hours, around the clock.

Somehow, my gut feeling told me that Natalie would be a candidate for preterm labor. Sure, one could blame her incompetent cervix, but in Natalie's case, I felt there was something more. All I could do was watch her very closely, continue the medication to stop the uterus from contracting, and assess her cervix at regular intervals. To do that, I need Natalie's cooperation. She was an intelligent young woman and most certainly understood the risks. Yes, the intercourse episode may have played some role, but I could not convince myself it was the main culprit.

The following day, Natalie attended for her regular visit. I asked Renee, our nurse, to accompany Natalie to my office, since I wanted to talk to her before her prenatal visit. Natalie greeted me cordially.
"I have been a good girl. My husband is sleeping in another bedroom," she said, smiling.
"I am sure that will help," I replied, and continued to voice my concerns over the risk of preterm labor. She was only twenty-five weeks. We had to avoid preterm labor by all possible means. I wanted to do an ultrasound, find out how her cervix was, and make

some decisions. I told Natalie she might have to be hospitalized for some time if the uterus continued to be irritable or to contract. "How long can we postpone preterm labor?" she asked. "All I can say is that we will try for as long as we can," I replied. "What would be a safe time to deliver the baby?" she asked. "Thirty-four weeks would be good, but we'll take whatever we can."

I subsequently performed an ultrasound and found that, indeed, Natalie's cervix was slightly more open than before, but the membranes were not protruding. The stitch I had put around the cervix during the cerclage was holding well, for the time being. There were no other problems. I monitored her uterus for about thirty minutes. It was an irritable uterus, with very low intensity contractions. I asked Natalie to limit her activities to a minimum and stay home, if not in bed, or in a recliner or something similar. I also increased the dose of her medication. I wanted to see her weekly or at any time if she began to feel contractions, particularly any recurring at regular intervals of less than twenty minutes. I also asked her to call in-between office visits to update me with her status.

Two more weeks passed without major problems. She was now almost twenty-eight weeks. Not ideal, but good enough if events forced us to deliver early. On the exact day she turned twenty-eight weeks, she called to tell me she was contracting. Her husband was with her and I asked them to come immediately to the emergency room. I also alerted the emergency physician to notify me as soon as she arrived.

Twenty minutes later, ER called to alert me that Natalie had arrived and that she was uncomfortable. I went right there and ordered an intravenous solution to be started, with medication to stop or slow down contractions.

Using the portable ultrasound, I took a look at her cervix. Membranes were beginning to be seen inside the partially opened cervix. Within a short time, Natalie was admitted to the high-risk obstetrical unit. Constant monitoring of her uterus began and her medication was increased. I also had Natalie in what is known as "Trendelenburg position"—lying flat on the back with the feet higher than the head by about thirty degrees. Gravity then tends to push the membranes backwards, inside the uterus, rather than allowing them to extrude through the partially opened cervix. This lowers the risk that membranes may rupture, which would force us to intervene and would increase the risk of infection.

Natalie found the position slightly uncomfortable. I explained to her why we needed to do this. She did not like being confined to the bed for the time being either. But, to her credit, she understood and said, "Whatever you say, doc."

Because the risk of preterm delivery was quite high, we also administered a drug that speeds the maturity of the baby's lung, which would minimize the risk of the premature infant developing breathing problems.
"Will my baby be delivered early?" Natalie asked me.
"Not if I can avoid it, Natalie. At twenty-eight weeks, infants fair quite well, but we still prefer to keep them in the uterus longer," I told her. I left the room, informing Natalie and her husband that I would be back in about an hour to see how the uterus was responding to medication. I also reassured them I was in the hospital, less than five minutes away from Natalie's room.

I was pleased to see that the medication soon slowed the uterine contractions significantly, reducing them from occurring every fifteen minutes, to about thirty to forty minutes apart. Natalie could not feel them. I was optimistic, and I shared my optimism with them. However, I also informed them that Natalie was here for a long stay, most likely until delivery.

The night was quiet. The monitor showed only an occasional contraction. The ultrasound showed no further changes in the cervix, and the membranes had retracted inside the uterus. I was very pleased.
"When can I stop lying upside down?" Natalie asked.
I told I would like her to remain like that for a further twenty-four hours. Then, slowly, we may attempt to adopt a more comfortable position.

"When can I get out of bed?" she asked.

"Don't push it," I said. "We'll see, as days go by, how you are doing. Fair enough?"

"I do not seem to have a choice, do I?"

"You are right," I told her.

"This kid starts giving me grief even before it is born," she said, smiling.

"Welcome to parenthood."

Natalie continued to improve. As promised, each day I started lifting up her head, a little bit at a time. I checked her cervix and the status of her membrane; they did not protrude for a few days but by day four, when she was almost flat on her back, they were back in the cervical canal. Unfortunately, we had to return to an upside down position to have the membranes retract again. This time, Natalie did not protest. "The baby is more important than my discomfort," she said. Her husband gave her a kiss. I replied, "Yes, it is."

The baby was growing comfortably. Since Natalie's contractions had subsided, I started lowering the dose of the medication she was receiving, but I maintained a basal level to keep any further uterine irritability in check. Unfortunately, I could not completely remove Natalie from the Trendelenburg position, but it was more tolerable and she was not complaining. The cervix was slightly open, but the suture still seemed to hold. By then, several weeks had passed since Natalie had first been admitted. We were just a day away from thirty-three weeks.

I remember going to make my rounds that morning. Natalie told me she'd had a good night, but that woke up quite uncomfortable. "Same contractions," she said. "I guess I need to be on the medication again."

Prior to my arrival, the nurse had placed the monitor on Natalie's abdomen. A quick look at the type of contractions told me they were far from being "the same." Their intensity and pattern indicated she was in labor.

"Natalie," I said, "these contractions indicate you are in full-blown labor. I believe this is the day. We should be OK. We are at thirty-three weeks."

I asked the nurse to bring in the ultrasound equipment. A quick view showed the cervix was opening and the membranes were now in the vagina. It was time to remove the suture we had placed during the cerclage, so that it would not tear the cervix. The nurse brought in the necessary instruments while I was explaining what we are going to do.

"It will not hurt you," I reassured Natalie. "It is like a pelvic exam. It will not take more than a couple of minutes."

The nurse was assisting me and focused the light so I had a clear view of Natalie's cervix. I grasped the string and, with a straight clip of the scissors, I snapped the suture.

"All done," I told Natalie. While doing the pelvic examination, I could feel the membranes were tense, and I could feel the baby's head high up behind the membranes.

I asked the nurse to call Natalie's husband and tell him she was in labor and would deliver that morning. I had to see another patient who had just been admitted, but I told Natalie I would be right there in labor and delivery. On walking out, I asked the clerk to call neonatology and alert them there was a baby of thirty-three weeks gestation to be delivered soon. I then entered the room of my other patient, who was in early labor. As I was talking to them, the intercom buzzed and Clarisse, the nurse taking care of Natalie, said simply and calmly, "Need you here immediately. I believe we have a prolapse."

I immediately ran to Natalie's room. Her water had just broken and the baby's heart had suddenly dropped to sixty beats per minute from a normal rate of one hundred and forty. I immediately put on a glove and examined Natalie vaginally. Sure enough, I could feel the baby's umbilical cord in the vagina and its head behind, pushing the cord against Natalie's pelvic bones. I gently pushed the baby's head upwards and, immediately, the heartbeat returned to normal. I looked at the clock on the wall. It was 9:15 am.

A prolapsed cord, which means the baby's umbilical cord has dropped into the vagina, is always an emergency of utmost priority. When the cord drops into the vagina, it usually becomes compressed. As a result, the cord blood flow is interrupted and the baby's heartbeat instantly drops to dangerously low levels. One only has minutes to correct this occurrence. A vaginal examination not only confirms the diagnosis, but also has to relieve the pressure on the cord so that its flow will not be impeded; otherwise, the baby will die or be severely damaged from a lack of oxygen.

I immediately told Natalie what was happening and that we needed to do an emergency cesarean section. Then I told Clarisse to have someone hold the head up while I prepared for an emergency cesarean section. By that time, two other nurses entered the room. One told me she had already alerted the neonatal service and called anesthesia. I was also told that the scrub nurse, my assistant, was on her way.

Nancy, one of the nurses, came in to replace me in holding up the head. As soon as she was gloved and sat on the bed, I rapidly removed my hand and she inserted hers.
"I've got it," she said, meaning she had the baby's head pushed up, away from the cord. "Cord's pulsating normally," she added.
From the time I had removed my hand to the time Nancy took my place, the baby's heartbeat did not show any decrease whatsoever.

As I left Natalie's room to scrub up, two of the nurses moved Natalie's bed toward the operating room, with Nancy sitting on the bed with her hand holding the baby's head up the entire time. Intermittently, Nancy would give a brief report: "We are OK here."

I changed into surgical scrubs, put on a mask, and scrubbed my hands and arms. Natalie was already on the table, and Nancy was by the table, still reassuring us, "We are OK here."
The neonatologist and two neonatal nurses were preparing their equipment, and the anesthesiologist was placing electrocardiograms sensors on Natalie chest, and an oxygen mask on her face.

"Breathe deeply," the anesthesiologist told her.

The scrub nurse handed me my sterile gown, which I put on rapidly. While the circulating nurse was tying my gown in the back, I put on my surgical gloves. The scrub nurse helped me drape Natalie's abdomen and when done, I told the anesthesiologist, "Let's go!"

Natalie was under anesthetic in no time. As soon as I was told Natalie was asleep, I opened her abdomen and made a uterine incision. Without any difficulty, I delivered the baby. It was a boy. After cutting his cord, I handed the baby to the attending neonatal nurse. The operating room clock read 9:27 am. It had taken us exactly twelve minutes from the time we declared the emergency to the time of the baby's birth.

"Thank you, Clarisse. Thank you, Nancy," I said. "Thanks to everybody. You were all great."

The infant cried immediately, and the neonatologist told me the baby was fine. I removed the placenta, and closed the uterus and abdomen. By 9:40 am, I was done. The anesthesiologist told me Natalie was also OK, with no problems there.

By that time, Natalie's husband was waiting in her room. As soon as I finished, I went to talk to him and tell him what happened. "Natalie is going to be in recovery room for a while. As soon as she is awake, you are welcome to go and see her. One of the nurses will take you there."

He thanked me, and asked when he could see the baby. I made arrangements for someone from the neonatal unit to take him to see his son while I visited Natalie in the recovery room.

Natalie was awake, but still groggy. I checked her vital signs sheet: normal. When Natalie was able to speak clearly, the first thing she asked was, "How's the baby?"

I reassured her that the baby boy was healthy.

Her husband entered the recovery room and gave her a kiss. "It's a beautiful baby," he told her. "He's fine."

About an hour later, Natalie was back in her room, alert and smiling. "We did it," she said. "I'm happy."

Natalie's course after surgery was perfectly routine. By the fourth day, she was ready to go home. Her baby remained in the neonatal unit, but after a few weeks, he went home too.

I never felt better

The majority of women who get pregnant are healthy, and most pregnancies are routine. The combination of healthy mother and normal pregnancy is the perfect blend for a healthy child. Unfortunately, there are always exceptions. Sometimes, complications develop in otherwise healthy women, or pregnancy occurs in a woman who had an existing, usually chronic, disease.

When I first saw thirty-year-old Alice, she was barely six weeks pregnant. She had been referred to me because she had been suffering from rheumatoid arthritis since the age of twenty-three. Rheumatoid arthritis is a chronic, usually debilitating, disease characterized by inflammation of the joints. The intricacies of the disease are quite complex. Ultimately, the joints become deformed and the pain and swelling is significant. In a large number of patients, pregnancy improves the symptoms of the disease. Hormonal changes associated with pregnancy, as well as certain immunologic factors, are thought to be the reason for this improvement.

Seven years of this disease had taken its toll on Alice, but she was able to continue her usual activities despite her discomfort. Her joints, particularly in her hands, had suffered the most. Periods of discomfort and pain alternated with periods of temporary relief. Alice's pregnancy was unplanned, and now, here she was, pregnant and worried.

Alice and Greg, her husband, readily expressed their concern about Alice's disease but also wanted to know how it might affect the infant. Was it safe to continue the pregnancy? Her discomfort was minimal at that time, and her medications seemed to be working.

We talked at length about their concerns. Alice was still quite early in her pregnancy and miscarriages are reported at slightly higher rates in patients with rheumatoid arthritis. Short of that, none of the common complications of pregnancy were more frequent in rheumatoid arthritis patients. What's more, I indicated, it is not unusual for the disease to improve as a result of pregnancy.

Postpartum, however, it is also common that symptoms recur. The medication she was taking did not pose any threat to her baby, but I asked her to let me know if there were any changes and cautioned that she should not start any new therapy before I had a chance to ensure it was acceptable during pregnancy. Altogether, I was optimistic Alice would have a routine pregnancy.

Alice continued to be apprehensive about the possibility of a miscarriage, but as the days went on, she freed herself of that fear and began to enjoy her pregnancy. Ultrasound examinations showed a perfectly healthy male infant. She was pleased. By Thanksgiving, Alice and Greg wanted to go and visit her parents. She was twenty weeks pregnant by then and I could see no problem with them driving a few hours to her parents' home.

Alice came to see me upon her return. Since she had become pregnant, other than the mild discomfort from her rheumatoid arthritis, she had been healthy. She had never had five months of uninterrupted relief from her disease before, and she was in awe, but strangely, she was also perturbed. She could not explain why. "Could it be that I transferred my disease to my baby, and that is why I have been feeling so good?" she asked.
I reassured her there was no such a thing as "transferring" such a disease.
She listened carefully and simply said, "I see."
Unsure what was troubling her, I probed a little further into her potential fears, but she did not react. Under usual circumstances, I would have asked her to return in two or three weeks. Instead, I asked her to return in one week. Somehow, I had the feeling there was more to her question, something that, for some reason, she did not want to discuss.

A week later, Alice was in my office again. The pregnancy was progressing uneventfully and she told me she was feeling fine. In fact, since being diagnosed with rheumatoid arthritis, she had never felt better. She was not sleeping very well, but by day she felt "hyper," as she put it. "I feel so well, I could cry," she said unexpectedly. "I owe my well-being to my baby."

Most patients understand that pregnancy may influence a given disease for better or for worse. In Alice's case, it seemed that knowledge had a significant psychological impact, well beyond "I am feeling good." I was concerned she may not fully realize it was a temporary relief. I needed to ensure that fact was clear in her mind, and that after delivery, when her symptoms recurred, she would not blame the child.

After her routine prenatal visit, I told Alice I wanted to talk further to her. I revisited her prior comment about "owing her well-being to the baby." Did she fully understand that, after delivery, the disease would likely recur?
Alice seemed surprised by my question. "Of course," she said, "that was my understanding".
I inquired as to how she felt about "being well."
"A blessing," she replied. "I feel that I owe this to my son, and I will never be able to love him enough for that. I just hope I will be well long enough to take care of him."
I must confess that this was the first time I had seen such an unconditional bond between an expectant mother and her unborn child. Whatever my concerns had been, they vanished. I was happy for that. But mostly, I was happy for Alice.

Taking care of Alice for the rest of her pregnancy was a delight. She went into labor a few days before her due date and delivered a healthy seven-pound baby boy. They named him Asher, which, I was told, means "blessed" in Hebrew.

* * *

Just give me a hug

Diabetes is a disease known from antiquity and takes its name from Latin and Greek words, to mean, essentially, "excessive urine." Diabetic urine, in addition to being excessive, also has the characteristic of being sweet; hence the name "mellitus," meaning "sweetened with honey," was attached to the disease's name in the seventeenth century. Over the centuries, diabetes was a death sentence. Only very mild diabetics would usually have survived to early adulthood. The disease's association with the function of the pancreas was not established until the mid-nineteenth century. The lack of insulin, the endocrine hormone responsible for the disease an produced by the pancreas, was not discovered until 1921 by two Canadians: Banting and Best:

Prior to the discovery of insulin, diabetic mothers were unlikely to get pregnant; if they did, they risked their lives. Chances were, the infant would die before birth. Infants who survived usually weighed more than nine or ten pounds at birth, making the birth traumatic for both mother and infant. Shortly after birth, these infants suffered severe respiratory problems and many died or had life-long residual health issues. Furthermore, congenital abnormalities, particularly of the heart, were common, which further jeopardized an infant's survival.

Progress in the management of mothers with diabetes was slow. In the last thirty years significant progress has been made in understanding the disease and its relation to pregnancy. Tight control of the mother's blood sugar levels significantly improved the infant's outcome and improved the chances for diabetic mothers to have a healthy child. Today, even the most severe of diabetic mothers has an excellent chance of having an uncomplicated pregnancy and a normal infant.

Thus, when Jessica came to our office for care, a diabetic since age seven, we reassured her that, with good control and close supervision, she should be able to have a normal pregnancy and a healthy infant.

At age twenty-five, this was Jessica's first pregnancy. She and her husband were excited about having a baby. Over the years, Jessica's diabetes had ups and downs—not unusual in those who become diabetic very early in life. Diabetes is a disease that turns a sufferer's life upside down, and this is particularly true for juvenile diabetics. They must lead a regimented life and it is not easy for them to keep up with their non-diabetic peers. As a result, frustration and rebellion are common. This usually leads to poor control of their diabetes, multiple hospitalization, and trips to emergency rooms for either very low or very high blood sugar, both of which can be life threatening. Jessica was no exception. Poor control over her teen years had taken some health tolls. Jessica was heavily overweight, which did not help her diabetes, and she had some damage in her vision which improved following laser eye surgery. To her credit, Jessica was now in excellent control of her diabetes—a reassuring situation.

In spite of her history, I was optimistic about Jessica's chances of having a healthy baby, and I shared my thoughts with Jessica and her husband. She was about twelve weeks pregnant when she first came to see me.

Her first ultrasound showed a normal infant and confirmed the gestational age. Jessica had a consultation with our dietician, who devised a correct diet for her, and we adjusted some of her insulin. After performing a physical examination, which was unremarkable, we rescheduled for her to return in two weeks.

At her next visit, I was pleased to see that Jessica was still carefully controlling her diabetes, and I congratulated her on that achievement. She told me that becoming pregnant had boosted her morale and that she intended to have perfectly well-controlled diabetes for the duration of her pregnancy.

At twenty-four weeks gestation, I performed an ultrasound to make certain her baby did not have any heart abnormalities, as some infants of diabetic mothers do. I was happy to be able to tell her that her infant had a perfectly normal heart.

Occasionally, Jessica's husband would attend office visits, which took place weekly. He and I had long chats about how well Jessica was doing. Their excitement grew with the progress of her pregnancy and her diabetes could not have been under better control.

At thirty-two weeks gestation, we started performing non stress testing, biophysical profiles and cord blood flow studies. These tests, when normal, are an indication of the infant's good health. Science still does not fully understand the profound effect diabetes can have on unborn infants. Therefore, the care of a diabetic mother requires rigid and close supervision to constantly evaluate the infant's well-being

When we were approaching the last few weeks of pregnancy, we decided on a delivery date that was about ten days before her due date. Experience has taught obstetricians that infants of diabetic mothers do not fare well if left undelivered after their due date. The general consensus is that delivery should be accomplished seven to ten days prior to expected due date.

In addition to our weekly tests, Jessica was taught to count the baby's movements, twice a day for an hour, and report any changes that might occur. Movement is a sign of infant well-being, while a change in the number or intensity or movements can be a red flag that not all is well with the child.

Three days before her baby was to be delivered, Jessica visited my office in the morning for her regular tests. The tests were fine and Jessica had no complaints. She was looking forward to her scheduled delivery.

Later that afternoon, Renee, our nurse, came into my office to tell me that Jessica had called to report that she had not felt the baby move since she had returned home, two hours before.
"I told her to come right in," Renee said. "I hope that was OK."
"Absolutely." I had just seen her just a few hours before, so it was hard for me to believe something had happened to her baby, but I told Renee to put a monitor on Jessica as soon as she reached the office, and to let me know.

An hour later, Renee entered my office again. "Jessica is here," she said. "I believe we have problems."

I looked at Renee, a first-class, experienced nurse. Tears filled her eyes. She did not need to say anything more: I knew.

Jessica was in the monitoring room, her husband tightly holding her hand. "What's going on?" she asked.

"Not sure yet," I answered as I fiddled with the monitor, unsuccessfully trying to relocate it several times. Jessica was overweight, and I hoped against hope that her size was making picking up the fetal heart rate difficult. Deep down, I knew I was fighting a losing battle. I asked Renee to wheel in the portable ultrasound machine so I could visually look for fetal heart motion. Without a word, she did so. Throughout her pregnancy, Jessica had established a close rapport with everybody in the office, from receptionists, to nurses, to secretaries. Over forty weeks, obstetrics staff usually come to know everybody quite well, but Jessica's personality had captured the hearts of everybody. Soon, word spread through the office that Jessica's baby had a problem. Silently, everyone lined the corridor, awaiting news. I could hear them thinking, *God, not Jessica's baby!*

But it was true. The ultrasound confirmed the dreaded news: the heart showed no motion. Jessica's baby had died somewhere between her morning office visit, when everything was well, and the time she had returned home. Once more, diabetes had played dirty tricks, right under our watchful eyes. I had no clue why.

I had great difficulty sharing the news with Jessica and her husband. She cried silently as her husband hugged her, and soon the two were crying in each other's arms. They stayed like that for a while. Renee, too, had tears in her eyes; I was fighting mine. One by one, in silence, the office crew from the corridor peeked briefly into the room, tears also in their eyes, and then returned to their desks. When I could speak clearly, I said, "I am so sorry, Jessica. I don't know what to tell you right now."

"You don't have to tell me anything. Just give me a hug," she said. I did.

The next day, Jessica delivered a stillborn baby boy. The child's appearance gave me no clue about the cause of death, so I asked Jessica and her husband if they would allow an autopsy. I also asked them what arrangements would be made for the baby. They agreed to the autopsy and told me that the baby would have a funeral and be buried.

The autopsy did not shed any new light on the cause of death, nor did the study of the afterbirth. On the day of the funeral, our office was closed for the morning. Everybody was present at the funeral service.

That child's death reminded me again just how much more we have to learn about this disease. Although we have made significant progress in the management of diabetic pregnancies, we must not forget that maternal blood sugar is only a symptom. Diabetes is much more than just high blood sugar. The body's entire vascular system is affected by diabetes; that is why some diabetics lose their sight, have to have legs amputated, or have heart disease or kidney disease. In pregnancy, the connection between the mother and her infant is achieved through the placenta, or afterbirth—a highly vascular and complex organ through which the baby receives oxygen and nutrients, eliminates its metabolic waste, and much more. The placenta also protects the infant by allowing only certain substances to reach the baby. It is vital to the survival of the infant before birth; however, its complexity is still not fully understood, and much of its normal function is yet to be determined. Consequently, the effect of diabetes on this vital organ still eludes us. Events like the loss of Jessica's baby are a tragic reminder of the research that still needs to be undertaken in this area.

Six months later, Jessica became pregnant again. This time, her pregnancy had a happy ending and we all attended the infant's baptism—a much happier occasion.

* * *

When the heart fails

A heart attack during pregnancy used to be extremely rare. An obstetrician could go through an entire career without ever having to take care of a pregnant woman who had a heart attack. In the past thirty years or so, many women have postponed having a baby until later in life, due to career choices or other personal reasons. It is now not unusual for a woman in her forties to become pregnant. As the age of future mothers increases, certain complications, such as hypertension or diabetes, for example, have become more common. Heart attacks, rarely seen in younger pregnant women, are not uncommon in older pregnant women. We also know that in addition to age, other factors intrinsic to pregnancy make a woman more prone to suffering a first heart attack during pregnancy. During pregnancy, the mother's total blood volume increases by about 40%, which creates an extra workload for the heart. Also, hormonal changes that occur during pregnancy may affect the heart.

Heart attacks during pregnancy tend to be more severe, for reasons we do not fully understand. There are also questions as to whether the standard treatments for heart attacks are always applicable to pregnant women. The risk of death for a pregnant woman having a heart attack, compared to non-pregnant patients, is probably two or three times higher. There is a lot still to be studied in this area. At the present time, conservative treatment is still the best we have.

Joanne, a thirty-eight-year-old pregnant woman, arrived at the ER complaining of shortness of breath, sweating, and feeling a heavy weight pressing on her chest. It did not take the ER physician long to diagnose that Joanne was having a heart attack. Appropriate emergency measures were taken and she was transferred to the coronary intensive care unit. The cardiologist in charge called me for an obstetrical consultation. I arrived to the coronary unit a few minutes later and was told that Joanne was relatively stable and that no decisions had yet been made about the course of her treatment.

It was Joanne's third pregnancy, and she had enjoyed entirely uncomplicated pregnancies before. Now twenty-nine weeks pregnant, she had not been aware of any problem earlier during this pregnancy either. I requested fetal monitoring to evaluate the baby's heart rate. When a mother suffers a heart attack, one of the problems is a decrease in her oxygen level. A low maternal oxygen level will decrease the oxygen available to the infant. Joanne's oxygen level was 90%, on the low side of normal. The infant's heart rate was steady at a rate of one hundred and thirty beats per minute. I also performed an ultrasound, which confirmed that the infant was indeed twenty-nine weeks. The cord blood flow was normal, as was the amount of amniotic fluid. Joanne was not having any contractions. At that point in time, from an obstetrical point of view, she was okay. As for her oxygen level, she was receiving oxygen. Without any further complications, her oxygen level would return to the high nineties and therefore the infant would have a normal oxygen level.

Joanne's medical history showed her to have been diagnosed with mild chronic hypertension two years ago, for which she was being treated with two drugs: one a calcium channel blocker, and the other a beta-blocker. These were very effective drugs that controlled hypertension by different mechanisms. Using a combination of drugs with different mechanism of action has proven to be one the most effective ways to control hypertension. Joanne had never had any heart problem. She had an EKG a year prior to this admission, and, as far as she knew, it had been normal. Her medical history revealed no other medical problems.

I asked Joanne for permission to request transfer of her medical records from another hospital to us. I also reassured her that, as of that moment, the infant appeared to be doing fine. Hopefully, she would not go into premature labor, which some women do following a heart attack. Should she go into premature labor, we would try to stop it with medication given intravenously. Even if the infant were to be born prematurely, the chances of survival at twenty-nine weeks gestation were good.

I asked the cardiologist if I could have an obstetrical nurse come to the cardiac unit and place a fetal monitor on Joanne. It would give us a constant record of the baby's heart and would monitor the uterus for contractions. It would also alert us if premature labor threatened.

The cardiologist had no objection to what we needed to do. He also told me that Joanne would have an echocardiogram in the next hour to assess damage to her heart. An echocardiogram, or echo for short, allows a visual evaluation of the heart, not only for its function but also for potential damage. A cardiac catheterization may have also to be considered. I asked him to please keep me informed of her cardiac condition. I had no objection to the cardiac catheterization, if needed. I also asked him to make sure that Joanne's abdomen was shielded during the procedure, to protect the infant from potential indirect radiation. Since the radiation during a catheterization would be mostly directed to Joanne's heart, in the chest, the radiation to the fetus would be minimal. The shielding of her abdomen would further protect the baby from indirect radiation from the equipment.

As I was about to leave the unit, David, Joanne's husband, arrived. Understandably, he was a nervous wreck. They were from out of town and he had some business in the area, so Joanne had traveled with him. She had been alone in the hotel when she had started feeling unwell and had called the concierge, who immediately called 911. The ambulance had brought her to the hospital.

The cardiologist asked David and me to join him in a small conference room. He explained Joanne's status to David and reassured him that Joanne had probably passed the critical period and that she was responding well to the treatment she was receiving. He also told him about the echocardiogram, which would enable them to determine whether a coronary stent may be needed to keep a blocked artery open or whether cardiac bypass surgery may be a better route. For my part, I reassured David that the infant seemed to be unaffected. Hopefully, Joanne would not go into premature labor.

"What if she goes into premature labor?" David asked.

"We will attempt to stop it. Should we not be able to do so, at

twenty-nine weeks, the infant has a good chance of survival."
He seemed more at ease. I gave him my card with a contact
telephone number, and also told him the name of my partner, who
would share Joanne's care with me.

The next few days were uneventful. Joanne was stable. Her echo
showed an area of the anterior wall of the heart with poor motion,
indicating that was where the lesion was. Joanne underwent a
cardiac catheterization that same day, and a stent was placed in
the blocked artery, reinstating a normal blood flow. The infant
remained fine throughout all these therapies. The cardiologists
were optimistic and fully expected to be able to discharge Joanne
within days.

On the eve of her expected discharge, Joanne started having
contractions. They were quite mild and irregular at first, but of
enough concern that I asked the cardiologist not to discharge her
the following day as planned. He agreed.

In spite of what appeared to be mild contractions, an ultrasound
showed that Joanne's cervix was changing. It was shorter than it
had been during my initial observation. Medication was started
in an attempt to decrease uterine activity as much as possible. It
appeared to work, but contractions did not subside entirely. I had
to continue to try to control the uterine activity while making sure
too much fluid was being administered; too much fluid could create
a fluid overload that Joanne's heart would not be able to handle,
which could result in cardiac failure.

We continued like that for a full twenty-four hours. Her heart
appeared to tolerate our management well, but her uterus remained
irritable despite the medication. Regardless, it did not reach the
pattern of full labor. The best I can say is that we were in limbo.
We could not discharge her, but she was not going into labor either.

Since the cardiologists did not think she needed to stay in the
intensive care unit, we transferred her to the labor and delivery
area. I had a conference with the cardiologist and told them that
should she go into labor, her cardiac status had to be monitored

very closely throughout labor and immediately postpartum. If she went into labor, we would have to transfer her back to the intensive care unit for cardiac monitoring and bring everything there to deliver her while she was being monitored. The cardiologists agreed with me that cardiac monitoring, so soon after a heart attack, was the right approach. "We haven't had a delivery in cardiology for some time," one of them kidded.
"Hope we won't have to do it," I answered.

For three consecutive days, we watched Joanne's uterus fluctuate between no contractions and mild contractions. One of the cardiologists was coming daily to check on her status. They were pleased with her cardiac condition.

We have also consulted with the neonatology service, to keep them updated on the possibility of having to deliver a twenty-nine week, now almost thirty-week, baby.

During the days that Joanne was in labor and delivery area, we had several meetings with our nurses, rotating through all shifts, to discuss a potential delivery in the cardiac unit. Everybody was up to date with how we would proceed, and what each person had to do. Delivery outside the labor and delivery area presents some logistical problems, which though not insurmountable, require careful planning. We did not want to have to use the protocol for an unexpected, emergency delivery. This was something different: an improvised labor and delivery room transported to the cardiac unit. Instruments, monitoring equipment, medications, everything available to us in a normal delivery would be moved there. We also had a contingency plan should we need to perform an emergency cesarean section. In the labor and delivery area, we have our own surgical rooms. In the cardiac unit, we had to plan to either go to the central surgical area of the hospital or return to our operating rooms. We opted for coming back to our area; it was closer. Furthermore, the central operating rooms, depending on the time of the day, may be all occupied, and in an obstetrical emergency, we could not wait. We had a trial run, and it worked well.

Since we were planning cardiac monitoring for Joanne, it would be a matter of discontinuing her monitoring for the duration of the trip from the cardiac unit to our operating rooms, where she would be immediately reconnected to the monitors. A cardiologist would join us during the move, with resuscitation equipment if needed, and remain in our surgical area for the duration of the surgery. We also decided, together with the cardiologist, that after surgery, should it become necessary, Joanne would return to the intensive cardiac unit for her immediate postoperative follow-up.

I personally went to talk to the chief of anesthesia, too, so that department would know about it in advance. In case of an emergency, explanations would only delay us. Furthermore, this was an unusual case, and if anesthesia were to be involved, it was necessary for them to know.

Late in the afternoon of Joanne's fifth day in the labor and delivery area, she started contracting. She was obviously beginning her labor. I called the cardiologists and told them we would be moving Joanne back to their unit. We also called neonatology to let them know to expect a call from us once we were close to delivery. I asked the clerk to call the anesthesiologist on duty for labor and delivery, and let him know that we were moving to the cardiac unit. As labor advanced, Joanne was to receive an epidural anesthesia to avoid her having pain, which is stressful to the heart. Furthermore, we did not want her to have to push. Pushing during the final stages of labor is a significant effort for the heart, which we wanted to avoid. Literally, we were aiming for Joanne to not even know she was in labor, so that her heart remained perfectly stable.

Two of our nurses accompanied Joanne to the cardiac unit where the cardiologists were awaiting us. Joanne's cardiac status needed to be closely monitored throughout labor. She had to have both central and peripheral arterial monitoring sensors—one catheter in a peripheral artery and the other in the central, pulmonary artery in her chest. These were placed uneventfully. Her contractions were picking up and a pelvic examination showed her cervix to be four centimeters dilated. It was time for Joanne to receive her epidural anesthesia.

The anesthesiologist explained to Joanne what he was about to do and proceeded to insert, through a needle placed in Joanne back, a fine catheter all the way into the epidural space, the area around the spinal cord, where the anesthesia would block her pain. Through that catheter, Joanne was to receive the epidural anesthesia that would keep her pain-free until the baby was delivered.

By that time, David had arrived at the hospital. He was already aware of our plans. During the days that Joanne had been in labor and delivery, he had asked if it would not be better for her not to have to undergo labor at all, and asked why we could not just perform a cesarean section. This may appear to be the fast way to deliver, but for a cardiac patient, surgical trauma and the recovery period is much more stressful than delivering vaginally under perfectly controlled circumstances. A cesarean section would only be performed in an emergency, if the infant were suddenly and unexpectedly in a life-threatening situation. Otherwise, we do not do it because it would not be in the best interests of the mother.

Shortly after the epidural anesthesia was in place, Joanne was no longer feeling contractions. She was comfortable and chatting with David. The labor monitoring showed contractions were continuing uninterrupted. Sometimes, an epidural anesthesia can slow down labor; this was not the case here. The infant seemed to tolerate labor very well. Its heart rate was fine and the continuous, regular beep of the baby's heart reassured both Joanne and David that all was well.

Although we had not yet called the neonatology service, the neonatologist, Dr. Naegle, and his nurse entered the cardiac unit, bringing with them the equipment they would need. They talked to both Joanne and David and reassured them that the chances of the baby surviving, at thirty weeks, were very good. They were understandably pleased and hopeful. Dr. Naegle told me that he was on call, but he would be waiting for my call when delivery approached. I thanked him.

Joanne continued to labor at a steady pace. All of her monitoring, continuous electrocardiogram, and oxygen levels, were normal, which made us feel confident. I had to check in on other patients, so I asked the obstetrical nurse to let me know if there was a problem at any time.

I left the intensive cardiac unit for labor and delivery, where another patient had just been admitted in labor. Mrs. Chandler was close to term and her pregnancy had been complicated by diabetes. I examined Mrs. Chandler and found that while her contractions were very good, her cervix had only now started to thin out and open. It would be some time before I was needed. I explained to her that I was available, but that I had another patient in premature labor after a heart attack, who was now in the cardiac intensive care unit. Mrs. Chandler wished her well. I asked the nurse to keep me informed and told her that, should there be any timing conflict, she should call my partner who was covering for me until Joanne delivered.

After that, I went to the antepartum unit, where undelivered patients are hospitalized for complications, and reviewed the latest events. Everything was quiet, which pleased me.

Not knowing how long Joanne's labor would keep me busy, I decided to have a snack. An obstetrician eats in between contractions, if he can. I was headed towards the cafeteria when my pager started buzzing. It was the cardiac unit. I hurried to the first available hospital phone and called the unit. The cardiologist alerted me that Joanne's heart had suddenly become arrhythmic, meaning that instead of having regular rhythm, known in jargon as lub-dab, which imitates its regularity, Joanne's heart was now entirely irregular and difficult to count. The most common arrhythmia is one we all have at times: premature ventricular contraction, or PVC. Normal hearts have PVCs many times. Some people refer to them as "palpitations." That is not what Joanne had. She had developed an atrial fibrillation, which meant that her heart chambers, known as atria, had started to flutter rather than contract. In a heart that had just experienced a heart attack, it is one condition you do not want to see.

"We'll take care of it," the cardiologist told me, but I knew that was easier said than done. I went straight to the cardiac unit and asked the nurse to give me a glove so I could examine Joanne. Although this was not an acute emergency, the sooner we could deliver her, the better. To my surprise, I found Joanne cervix to be seven centimeters dilated. The baby's head had come down considerably. At thirty weeks, the infant would weigh no more than two and a half pounds, at most. As soon as the cervix opened, its head would come down into the pelvis and I could deliver it without delay by applying special forceps used in premature infants.

In spite of the arrhythmia, Joanne was stable and doing well. She had no complaints, no shortness of breath, no pain of any kind. The cardiologist had just administered some anti-arrhythmic medication. There were no worrisome changes in her monitoring devices. She and David were told what was going on and the cardiologist shared his concern, but he was positive that this event would not be of major significance for the duration of her labor.

Within the next hour, Joanne's cervix progressed to full dilation. I ruptured her membranes and clear amniotic fluid rushed out. As expected, the infant's head was now on the perineum. I asked the nurse to call neonatology and let them know we were ready to deliver. In the meantime, we made the necessary preparations for delivery. The epidural was holding Joanne very well. She had no feeling whatsoever on her perineum. Once I scrubbed my hands and put a gown and gloves, I took the forceps and gently applied one blade at a time on the sides of the baby's head. I asked the nurse to place her hand on Joanne's abdomen and let me know when the next contraction began. Unlike what most people seem to believe, the forceps is not an instrument to pull the baby's head down and out, but to allow the contraction to naturally push the baby down, while the forceps gently directs the head in the right axis for a safe delivery.

It worked beautifully, and the baby, a little girl, was delivered. After cutting the cord, I handed the infant to the neonatologist in attendance. The infant cried spontaneously and the neonatologist told us that the little girl was breathing on her own and needed no intubation. Good news! Her weight was two pounds, four ounces.

Both Joanne and David were happy. The neonatology team left with the baby and told David he could visit the baby in the neonatal intensive care unit. Shortly thereafter, the placenta delivered without any problems.

In patients with heart problems, the immediate post-partum period can be critical because of the loss of blood and the adjustments the heart has to make due to the sudden change in blood volume. But Joanne was comfortable and the anesthesiologist told us he would remove the catheter in a short while. He was still monitoring Joanne and she would remain in the cardiac unit until her arrhythmia resolved. Sometimes, such a resolution is spontaneous; other times, it may need intervention.

I called my partner to tell him that Joanne had delivered a healthy baby girl that had been transferred to the neonatal intensive care unit. I also asked him to please take care of Mrs. Chandler, who was in labor.

The next day, Joanne was apparently feeling quite well. She had slept all night and was feeling refreshed. When I went to see her, I looked at her EKG tracing, and to my pleasant surprise, found it perfectly normal. The atrial fibrillation converted entirely to a normal rhythm. While Joanne was not yet out of the woods, this was a very good step in the right direction.

After two more days in the cardiac unit, she was able to be moved back to the labor and delivery area. I was asked not to discharge her for another forty-eight hours. She was placed on daily oral medication in order to control a possible recurrence of her arrhythmia. Atrial fibrillation has a tendency to recur, particularly in a damaged heart. She was also placed on other medications for her heart, in addition to antihypertensive medication.

When Joanne arrived on our unit, I went to see her. She had no complaints and was looking and feeling well. We talked a while about her health and future care. The cardiologist did not want her to be on the road yet. They did not mind, since the little girl would not able to leave hospital yet either; she had to gain some weight and become stronger. They remained in town for another week, which allowed them to visit their daughter in the intensive care neonatal unit almost daily. Both parents were pleased with their daughter's progress and the neonatologist did not anticipate any long-term problems for the little girl.

At the end of the week, they left for home. David planned to come in a week later to see the little girl and make plans for her discharge from hospital. Joanne hoped that she could travel back to take her baby home, too.

"I was lucky," Joanne told me. "If it had to happen, I was lucky you and your staff were around to help me. Thanks a lot."
I put my hand on her shoulder and said, "It was a privilege taking care of you. Send me a picture from her first birthday."

Hospital by helicopter

One morning, I arrived at the hospital quite early and had just said good morning to the staff when the head nurse informed me we were expecting a patient who was being transported from one of our feeder hospitals, about one hundred miles away.

"She is coming by helicopter. She has twins at twenty-five weeks gestation, ruptured membranes, and is in early labor. Dr. Malone, her physician, is flying in with her."

What a way to start a morning! "OK," I said, "are they in the air already?"

"Not yet," the nurse replied. "There was some delay at the community hospital. I am not sure why."

"Please let me know as soon as they call," I asked.

"Will do"

At the antepartum unit, I made my rounds. We had about six patients in the hospital and everyone was apparently doing just fine. When the floor clerk came and told me labor and delivery was on the line, I picked up the phone to speak to the head nurse.

"They are in the air," she told me. Dr. Malone wants to talk to you."

"OK. Put him on."

The noise of the helicopter made reception difficult, but I understood that the patient had apparently ruptured her membranes early that morning. She had experienced some contractions, but they subsided and she was now comfortable. They agreed to ring ten minutes before the estimated arrival.

Sometime later, we received the call and two nurses and I prepared to meet them at the helipad—about one hundred yards from the emergency room entrance—with a gurney and an emergency delivery pack. The chopper appeared in sight in no time, and landed. Once its engines were shut down, we approached. Dr. Malone was the first to emerge. I greeted him and asked how the patient was doing.

"She seems to be OK. She rarely had contractions during the flight. Although your flight nurse came to pick her up, I thought, just in case, I should come to be available if needed."
"I understand," I replied.

Our two nurses, together with the flight nurse, brought the patient out. As soon as she was on the gurney, I introduced myself. "I am Dr. Aladjem, maternal fetal medicine specialist, I will be taking care of you."
"Nice to meet you," she said. "I am Roberta."
I asked her if she felt any contractions or discomfort, and she told me she had no pains at all. "Good," I answered, "our nurses will take you to labor and delivery, and I will be seeing you there shortly." I then asked Dr. Malone to join me in labor and delivery, where we could have a cup of coffee together.

Once in labor and delivery, we enjoyed coffee and donuts—which are rarely missing, no matter what the time of day it is. Dr. Malone was a family physician who was also practicing obstetrics, and over a period of years he had referred many patients to us. He was very conscientious about what he was doing, and never took on anything that was over his head. Twins at twenty-five weeks gestation with ruptured membranes was not something he would want to handle alone.

Cynthia, one of the labor and delivery nurses, entered the lounge to let me know that Roberta was in room four. I asked her to have the ultrasound equipment available.
"It's already there: she said, I introduced her to Dr. Malone and added that we would be there shortly.

Robert was a young woman of twenty-seven years, experiencing her second pregnancy. She greeted me and told me she did not expect to meet me so soon. Dr. Malone had already anticipated that she would be referred to our care, suggesting she should deliver in our hospital. Her chart from Dr. Malone's office indicated she had apparently had a normal pregnancy until then, and her first

111

pregnancy, two years ago, had been uneventful, with delivery at term. She had discovered she was carrying twins this time around at her first ultrasound, at about fifteen weeks. I asked if there are twins in the family, and she told me her husband was a twin.

I let Roberta know I would be performing an ultrasound, to see what was going on, and started scanning her abdomen to look at the first twin, situated in the lower part of her uterus. The amount of fluid appeared to be normal. Measuring this twin placed him at about twenty-four and a half weeks, which was consistent with the history. I viewed the second twin, in the upper part of her uterus, and its amniotic fluid was fine as well. This second twin was also consistent with her being twenty-four to twenty-five weeks pregnant. In fact, their measurements were very similar. Such findings were inconsistent with a history of ruptured membranes. I looked at the cervix, which appeared normal and closed. There was nothing else remarkable in my ultrasound

Dr. Malone told me that he had seen fluid in the vagina, which tested positive for amniotic fluid. "I don't understand," Dr. Malone said. "Could it be a high leak?"—meaning that the membranes of one of the twins may have had a small tear and leaked fluid, but not enough to decrease the amount of fluid in the amniotic sac. "Certainly that could be a possibility. We see that occasionally." In such cases, the leak usually seals or goes on to rupture completely; there is no way to predict which.

"The other possibility," I told Dr. Malone, "would be that only one of the membranes had ruptured." The sac in which the baby develops, called the amniotic sac, is composed of two membranes: one on the outside, called chorion, and another one in the inside, called amnion. These two membranes stick tight together for the duration of pregnancy and are referred to jointly as "membranes." If some amniotic fluid penetrates the space between the two membranes, the chorion may rupture and the amniotic fluid in that little sac will leak, just as if the two membranes had ruptured. However, it was not possible to make that diagnosis until we could determine that the fluid remained normal and that no further leakage would occur, in which case one may assume that this scenario had taken place.

"You mean we should not have come?"

"Not at all. Only further observation over a period of days will tell us what really happened. We have to go on the basis of your diagnosis of ruptured membranes. That, for the time being, is the safe thing to do. Time will tell whether we were right."

I asked Roberta whether she had followed our conversation or if she like for me to explain to her. She assured me she had fully understood. What I did not know, was that Roberta was a biology teacher in her hometown, so she had perfectly followed our conversation. "It's very interesting, I must say," she added. "How long will I have to be here?"

"At least a few days." We needed to follow this very closely, look for further leaks, repeat ultrasounds to reassess the amount of fluid in both sacs, and run a few other tests.

Roberta was satisfied and told us she would call her husband, who was at work and had been unable to accompany her. I told Roberta she was allowed to walk around the labor and delivery area, but that, should she at any time feel fluid from her vagina, she should return to bed immediately and let the nurse know.

Dr. Malone's cell phone buzzed. His ride was waiting by the emergency room. "I feel bad," he said.

"You shouldn't," I replied. "You absolutely did the right thing."

Had Roberta been my patient and presented at the hospital with her history, we would have done exactly what we are doing now."

'Thank you," he said. "Which way out?"

"I'll take you there." I said.

I returned to labor and delivery to find Cynthia had started monitoring Roberta. The recording was flat, indicating there were no contractions—an encouraging result. I reassured Roberta that there did not seem to be a problem and that we would know for sure in a couple of days.

Over the next three days, we performed repeated ultrasounds without noticing any change in the amount of amniotic fluid. She had no further leaking, and by the third day, I performed a vaginal examination. Her vagina showed no sign of amniotic fluid and was totally dry. During her walks, she never felt any leaking. Her lab tests were also all normal with no sign of a potential infection.

I told Roberta we were ready to discharge her, so she should call her husband to come and pick her up. We discussed her forthcoming delivery and I agreed with Dr. Malone that she should be delivered at our hospital. Because it is not unusual for twins to deliver early, I told her that, if she went into premature labor, she would absolutely need to be here. Furthermore, I knew Dr. Malone did not deliver twins.

I asked if she had any friends or family in the area and she did, so I suggested that it would prudent if, after thirty-two weeks, she settled near here to avoid a rush trip to our hospital when labor started. She did not anticipate any problems with that.

I discharged Roberta that afternoon. She thanked me and asked if, once she moved to town, I would see her for her prenatal care until she delivered.
"Absolutely" I told her. "It would be our pleasure.
After discharging Roberta, I called Dr. Malone and reported her progress, telling him that she would move closer for the final few weeks of her pregnancy. Dr. Malone thought that was a great idea and promised to keep me up-to-date about her progress.

Roberta had no more problems. Close to thirty-two weeks gestation, she moved in with some good friends and I saw her weekly until her delivery at thirty-six weeks. She had a boy and a girl, and we were all elated to have been able to deliver healthy thirty-six-week twins.

* * *

Mozart or rock and roll?

Shortly after finishing my rounds one morning, I left the obstetrical floor and went directly to my office. I knew we had a busy morning, so after changing into my office coat, I went to the nurse's desk to look at my schedule. There were five new patients, in addition to the usual revisits. Since my first patient was a new arrival, I decided to look at the note from the referring physician, which would give me an idea what to expect.

Dr. Giordano, the referring physician, had written a lengthy letter. Mrs. Sandra Thomas was a twenty-seven-year-old woman who had lost her first pregnancy, two years ago, at about twenty-four weeks gestation. Her infant, barely a one-pound little girl, had died shortly after birth. There had been no apparent reason for the very early delivery, and now she was pregnant again, so was being referred due to her history. What caught my attention in Dr. Giordano's letter was his comment that Sandra showed no interest whatsoever in her current pregnancy. Her statement to him was: "I got pregnant because my husband wanted a child." Dr. Giordano's assessment was that this attitude was likely the result of her previous loss. He felt that this information was important—and, most certainly, it was.

After losing a baby, most women become very cautious about their subsequent pregnancies. Their fear of losing the new pregnancy becomes their main focus. Usually, it subsides once the pregnancy has passed the time when the previous loss occurred. I had never before taken on a patient who showed no interest in her pregnancy, or who maintained she had become pregnant only because her partner wanted a child.

Sandra's appointment was at nine o'clock in the morning. She was on time and accompanied by her husband, Rick. When I entered the room and introduced myself, her husband stood up and greeted me, and introduced himself and his wife. Sandra did not say anything.

As usual, I started by telling them my understanding of why they were in my office. Rick did the talking. He confirmed the information Dr. Giordano had given me regarding their loss. I asked Sandra how far along she thought this pregnancy was. Rick answered that she was probably three months pregnant. Somehow, I had to put a stop to Rick answering my questions. I paused for a moment, looked at Rick, and as gently as I could, told him that Sandra would presumably become my patient, and while I appreciated his participation, I needed to get my answers from her.

He acknowledged that and looked at his wife. After a pause, Sandra finally told me her last menstrual period was two and a half months ago. "I really had no interest in becoming pregnant," she told me. "But Rick insisted we try again. So, here I am." She then turned her head slightly away from Rick and me.
"Mrs. Thomas," I continued, "I need to ask you a direct question, and I would appreciate a straight answer. Since you are pregnant, do you intend to receive your prenatal care in this office? I respect your loss, it was unfortunate, but now we have an entirely new pregnancy." She looked at me, and after a moment of hesitation, said, "Yes, I do."

I proceeded to ask questions about the circumstances regarding her previous loss. She appeared to have had an uneventful pregnancy until the morning she started contracting early, went to the hospital and, an hour after her arrival, delivered a premature little girl. No one could tell her why this happened. The girl died within hours of birth.

I told her I would like to perform an ultrasound, should she agree, and I would then examine her. Sandra had no objections. Rick accompanied us to the ultrasound examining room. It was an unusual experience. Generally, both mother and father are thrilled at seeing their baby for the first time. Rick was very interested, but Sandra showed no interest whatsoever. In fact, when I went to point out the baby, she said she would not know what she was looking at, and turned her head in the opposite direction.

116

When I had finished, I told them the nurse would come to accompany her to the examining room, and take Rick to my office. Her examination was normal. Since we were alone, I wanted to try to understand where she was coming from. I did not get very far. All she would tell me was that she did not really wanted to be pregnant, but Rick had insisted. Now that she was pregnant, she would go on with it, but she was not excited about the new pregnancy. I did not get the impression that this was a marriage on the rocks, but I knew that not everything was entirely positive. Obviously, she was depressed, but when I offered a referral to a counselor, Sandra flatly refused it.

After the examination, we met in my office. Rick seemed excited that everything was OK so far. He told me that he and Sandra had agreed to attempt another pregnancy, and he hoped that, as time went on, Sandra would change her attitude.

She received the usual prenatal instructions and I told her that if any of her lab tests were of concern, I would give her a call. We scheduled her next visit for three weeks time.

My assessment was that Sandra's care could become a challenge, particularly because I did not know the cause her first pregnancy loss. However, I could offer no intervention at that time other than close observation if something developed as Sandra's pregnancy progressed.

"Mrs. Thomas is a peculiar lady," the nurse said when she came into my office to tell me my next patient was ready. Like me, my nurse had never seen a patient so disinterested in her pregnancy. "Yes, she is," I replied.

As I was perusing the next patient's chart, I started thinking about Sandra. Her attitude was most unusual, so I was trying to understand her lack of interest. Couples often disagree as to the timing of a pregnancy, but it is generally worked out between them. In this case, Sandra had obviously gone along with Rick's desire for a baby. I concluded that maybe she *did* want a pregnancy, but was simply afraid of attempting one. Rick's insistence on trying for

117

a new baby most likely provided her with an unconscious excuse to attempt another pregnancy, while her lack of interest masked her fear of a repeat miscarriage. If the pregnancy succeeded, her apathy would hopefully change to delight, the usual reaction to a new baby. Should that not be the case, she could always say she did not want the pregnancy in the first place. It is amazing what the mind can do to a person! I left my office and went to see the next patient.

For the next couple of visits, nothing much happened. The baby was growing, as was to be expected, and there were no signs of anything concerning. At one visit, while examining her abdomen to assess the growth of the uterus, I felt the baby kick. Sandra did not react. I asked her if she had felt the baby move, and she denied it. Sandra was a woman of average weight. In obese women, sometimes fetal movements are not felt until later, because of the additional abdominal tissue, but this was not the case with Sandra. I asked if she had felt the baby move yet at all.
"No," came her answer.
That concerned me. There really was no way she could have missed that kick. I decided to do a brief ultrasound and asked if she would like to look at the screen. She hesitated. Then she said, "No, thank you."
When I asked her if she wanted to know the sex of the baby, she answered that she wanted to be surprised.

I was beginning to wonder whether Sandra might end up being a "pregnancy denial" case—a serious psychiatric disorder in which women deny they are even pregnant. Since we were now so close to the time when Sandra had lost her previous pregnancy, I decided to wait until the following visit to reassess the situation.

"You are fast approaching twenty-four weeks," I told her. "I am sure you will be relieved when that time has passed. So far, your pregnancy has been entirely normal, and I have no reason to think that anything unusual will happen at this time."
She paused for a long while, and then said, "I hope you are right."
That alone was somehow encouraging. It gave me reason to believe

that my initial assessment regarding her lack of interest may have been correct. I told her I would see her in two weeks, but that if there were any problems before then, she should let me know immediately. She nodded in agreement and left.

Only a week passed before Sandra called the office and wanted to talk to me. The nurse told her I was in surgery and could not talk at that time, but asked Sandra if she had a message that the nurse could relate it to me.
"No, thank you. I will wait for his call," Sandra had answered.

I returned to the office at around five in the afternoon and returned her call without delay. When Sandra answered the phone, I immediately asked her if she had any problems.
"Absolutely not," she said. She thanked me for returning her call and told me her good news: "The baby is kicking. I felt it all night, and feel it all the time."
I told her how pleased I was, and that I was looking forward to seeing her at her next visit. "I'll be there," she said, and hung up.

I thought we were finally out of the woods. For the first time, her voice sounded alive and I thought she was genuinely happy. I was pleased, above all, for her.

Four days later, Rick called. "Did you hear the news?" he asked.
"Yes, I did. I am happy for both of you," I answered.
He then proceeded to tell me that Sandra was spending her time in an armchair, counting the baby's movements constantly. Not only that, but she had read somewhere that babies liked to hear music before birth. She had purchased a small tape recorder and recorded all kinds of music, playing it to the baby through a small speaker she placed on her abdomen. She had also recorded a lullaby herself and was playing it to the baby so the infant could get used to its mother's voice. "Is she OK? Is all this normal?" Rick asked. "She has gone from one extreme to the other. I do not know what to do."

That is certainly a change, I thought. Her move away from her prior passivity and lack of interest was good, and it seemed that she was now happy. I told Rick that music would not harm the baby;

in fact, research indicates that babies react favorably to music, which can calm them down or increase their activity, depending on the type of music being played. Some people have theorized that hearing the mother's voice prior to birth is good for the baby, too. I did not see anything wrong with what Sandra was doing, but I asked Rick to keep me posted,

Sandra came to our office for her scheduled visit a week later. She was a changed woman. She was colorfully dressed, and she chatted to everybody in the office, telling them how happy she was to have felt the baby move. Apparently, she had researched the baby's reaction to music, too. "I am playing all kinds of music," she said. "I can tell what the baby likes or does not like. He loves Mozart." "How do you know?" I asked. "Because when I play rock and roll music, he kicks me very hard. With Mozart, he moves slowly. I don't think the baby likes rock and roll. I think it disturbs him." I could not argue with her. She could well be right. It was an interesting twist.

Obstetrically, Sandra was in excellent condition. We were approaching thirty weeks and sailing on without a glitch! By thirty weeks, I started seeing her every two weeks. She did not seem to have a care in the world. One morning, she called the office and told the nurse the baby had stopped moving. We brought her in that very same morning. Her examination was entirely normal, the infant was active, and our tests to assess any potential problems with the baby concluded that the infant was fine.

Babies have periods of activity alternating with periods of quietness. I reassured Sandra that nothing appeared to be wrong and we taught her how to correctly monitor her baby's activity, and when to be alerted that something may be wrong.
Still, Sandra was not happy. "How do I know that, from home to here, the baby won't die," she said, somewhat defiantly. I was beginning to think that that her prior indifference had turned into almost an obsession—and I had seen obsession before.

I reassured her the best I could and she reluctantly left the office. I was sure I would be hearing from her again soon. Sandra rang

again even sooner than I thought she would. As soon as she got home, she called the office. She told the nurse that we had told her she should feel no less than ten movements an hour, and she only felt nine. Was that normal?
The nurse did her best to reassure her. Then, the nurse had an idea. "Did you play some rock and roll music?" she asked Sandra.
"Good idea," Sandra replied.
An hour later, she called back and told our nurse that playing rock and roll worked.

Sandra had become something of a celebrity in our office. Staff called her "the rock and roll mother" until I called them to order. I could not allow them to have fun at the expense of a patient, least of all a patient with psychological problems that had arisen after the loss of her first baby. Everyone in my team was very caring, but they had to understand that this was not funny, even if it felt that way.

At every visit, Sandra showed some signs of calming down a little, although her level of anxiety was still significant. At times, we had long talks about her forthcoming delivery and what to expect. "Do you think we could have some music during delivery," she once asked.
I assured her that it was OK, and that if she wanted to bring her recorded music, she could play it. "But not rock and roll, please," I told her. "I am like your baby: I do not care for it much."
She started laughing and said, "Oh, I love it. Would you really mind?"
I reassured her I would be able to tolerate it if she liked it.

By thirty-four weeks, Sandra was having Non Stress Testing twice weekly. Non-Stress Testing is carried out by monitoring the baby's heart rate and correlating it to the baby's movements. With each movement, the baby's heart rate goes up and then comes back down to where it was. On a paper strip, the graph looks very much like a roller coaster, which is an indication of a healthy baby.

Sandra was looking forward to these tests. She was always apprehensive at the beginning, until we started picking up the baby's movements and the heart started going up and down. "Good baby," she used to say with each movement.

As the days and weeks went by, we got used to her calls from home, asking if this, or that, was normal. The nurse got to know her well and had the ability to put her at ease. Sandra would always tell the nurse what music the baby had been listening to that day, and the nurse became quite fond of her and looked forward to her calls. One day, when Sandra's call was late, the nurse actually called her to make sure everything was all right!
At her next visit, Sandra told me she had been really moved by the nurse calling her. "I feel good about your people," she told me.

She reached thirty-nine weeks, barely a week from her due date. The baby was moving less now, which was normal because by then it is beginning to descend into the pelvis, where its movements were restricted. This was, however, a very stressful time for Sandra, who was used to her baby's activity. Her baby's decreased activity was getting to her. Not even her rock and roll trick helped. Fortunately, before she reached forty weeks, Sandra went into labor.

She arrived at the hospital around four in the morning. It so happened that I had been on call, and as such, I was in the hospital. The night call had been an easy one, with only one delivery. When Sandra arrived in the labor and delivery area, the nurse told her she would call me, and to her amazement, I arrived just ten minutes later. I greeted both Rick and Sandra.
"I did not know you lived so close to the hospital," Sandra told me. I explained that I was on call so was already in the hospital. Sandra panicked; somehow, she had figured out that after a night on call, I would probably have to go home.
"You won't deliver me?" she asked, her voice trembling.
I understood her concern. Under normal circumstances, my partner would arrive to take over by eight in the morning, and I would leave. But I felt I could not do this to Sandra and reassured her that I would be taking care of her delivery, not to worry. "Thank you, sooooo much," she gushed.

I examined Sandra to find that she was indeed in labor. Her contractions were coming every four to five minutes, and were of good intensity. The baby's head was already applied against her cervix, which was soft and beginning to dilate. It would be a while before delivery would be imminent, and I shared that information with Sandra and Rick. Remembering that she wanted to have music during her delivery, I asked, "Did you bring your music with you?"
"Oh, you did not forget. Yes, I did. Can I?" she asked.
I updated the assigned nurse about Sandra's desire to have music during her delivery. "Wonderful," said the nurse.

As it turned out, they really came prepared. They had a mini tape player system with adjustable volume and a mini speaker attached for the baby. The nurse was delighted. "Music to deliver by," she said, smiling as I left the room.

By then, it was close to seven in the morning. I was hungry and tired, so I went to the cafeteria and ate a good breakfast. Sandra, I thought, would not deliver until late in the afternoon if everything worked well. By eight, my partner arrived and we discussed our shared patients.
"You're not to worry about Sandra. I will be taking care of her," I told him.

I was looking forward to taking a little nap before Sandra's labor got really active. Just in case, I returned to labor and delivery to tell them where they could reach me and to make sure everything was well. As I entered the delivery room, the clerk greeted me and asked if we are having a party in there.
"I don't think so. Why?"
"We have all this music floating around here," she told me.
"Oh, you mean Mrs. Thomas? Well, a little music won't hurt. It will keep all of you awake," I said jokingly. She laughed.

I went to Sandra's room. She was in labor but still comfortable. The music on the tape recorder was a Mozart concerto for piano and orchestra, also known as Elvira Madigan, after the movie of the same name in which it was the main musical theme. The mini-speaker was on her tummy so the baby could enjoy it too.

I told Sandra I would be in the hospital, but that the nurse would be able reach me as Sandra's labor progressed. "I doubt you will be ready to deliver until sometime this afternoon," I told her. I asked her again if she still wanted to have a natural childbirth, and she confirmed that she did. "Should you change your mind as labor progresses, please let the nurse know. Not a problem, anesthesia is only a phone call away." She nodded.

The doctor's rooms were just around the corner from labor and delivery. Before lying down, I called my wife to let her know I would not be home until later that day. I fell asleep in no time. When on night call, even one of relatively little activity, the interrupted sleep wears you down. I believe that part of a physician's training is to fall asleep in no time and recoup as many hours as one possibly can. It is a common jest in the profession that "obstetricians eat and sleep in between contractions." I was most certainly living proof of that.

The telephone woke me up. It was almost noon. I had managed a good three to four hours of sleep and felt quite refreshed. "You are wanted for Mrs. Thomas," the clerk said. I stood up, washed my face, put my coat on, and entered the delivery room. Sandra was far along in her labor by now. Her cervix was almost completely dilated, with the baby's head behind intact membranes. It was time to break her membranes. The nurse anticipated my intentions and asked me if I needed the membranes hook. I signaled that I did. The membranes hook is nothing but a sterile long plastic handle with a hook at its tip, which allows to "hook" the membranes and rupture them. There was no problem, and clear, warm fluid came through the vagina. I kept my hand inside the vagina for a few moments to ensure that the cord will not come down and be trapped between the head and the pelvic bones. The head accommodated itself and blocked the opening of the cervix, which by now was fully dilated.

"Nancy will start coaching you to push with each contraction," I told her. Nancy was the nurse now in charge of Sandra's care.

Rick, who was dozing in the armchair, stood up and asked me how things were going. I reassured him that everything was just fine, and that Sandra would be delivering soon. Judging by her progress, it should not take more than an hour or so.

Nancy started coaching Sandra how to push with each contraction. I heard Rick asking Sandra if she still wanted music. "Absolutely," she said, in between huffing and puffing. "Put some rock and roll on." Nancy smiled and told her, "You really came prepared." They both laughed.

It occurred to me that, considering Sandra's attitude towards her pregnancy when she first saw me, she had come a long way, music or no music. I was beginning to think it might not be a bad idea to have some piped music in labor rooms, just like we had in some operating rooms. I made a note in my mind to take it up with the administration.

As things were not yet in full swing, I went to the doctor's lounge for refreshments. I did not feel like a full lunch, but had my pick of salads, fruit, crackers and cheese in addition to beverages and coffee. My partner was there too and asked me how the "rock and roll mother" was doing. "She is starting to rock," I said smiling. "Another hour or so, and we'll be done."
He told me about a new patient he had seen in the office that morning. "Sadly, she has some serious problems. We need to talk about her tomorrow."

I ate some fruit and drank a cup of coffee, as I flipped through up a couple of medical journals from the table, but it was not long before my beeper buzzed again. It was labor and delivery.

Back in Sandra's room in labor and delivery, Nancy told me, "She's close."
The music player was blasting *Crocodile Rock* by Elton John. From the corner of my eyes, I saw Rick suddenly grow pale and sit down in the chair, his head between his knees.

125

"You're OK?" I asked him.

"I'll be OK," he whispered. "I won't pass out."

"You better not," Sandra told him, loud enough to be heard over the pumping music. A nurse cracked the door, peeked into the room and asked: "Is everything all right?"

Nancy made a dismissing sign with her hand, and the door closed again.

I almost felt like laughing. It looked as a scene from a Marx Brother movie. The music was blasting, the husband was in the chair, with his head between his knees, Sandra was pushing and huffing and puffing and pushing some more, Nancy was coaching Sandra, and I was looking at all that and asking myself: *is this for real?*

I examined Sandra. She was ready, so I told Nancy we were ready to deliver. She pressed the button on the wall that signaled an impending delivery and two new nurses entered. In less than thirty seconds, the labor room became a delivery room. Surgical lights descended from the opening ceiling, a surgical table appeared from nowhere with everything needed for a delivery, the front part of the bed disengaged from the rest, which became a delivery table. My surgical gown was on the surgical table. I washed my hands, put the gown on, and gloved up. By that time, the neonatal service was there too.

I examined Sandra again. The baby's head was down in the pelvis. It should be delivered within one or two pushes. I told Sandra to hold her breath with the next contraction and push down hard. Nancy was supporting her slightly elevated back to compound the pressure of the contracting uterus, and in no time, the baby was born. It was a nice healthy baby boy. I guess he weighed no less than eight pounds. The neonatal nurses took the baby, cleaned him, and returned him to his mother's arms. The neonatal nurses told Sandra that the baby was eight pounds, three ounces.

"APGAR nine and ten, Dr. Aladjem," they told me. It could not have been any better.

Rick was slowly getting back to normal and finally stood up to return to Sandra's side. "He is beautiful," Sandra told him. "He looks like you," Rick said.

The music had stopped and the tape was rewinding itself. Then it started all over again. Mozart's music, the Elvira Madigan piano concerto, filled the room. The baby was smiling.

* * *

SECTION 3:

THE MOMENT OF TRUTH

A matter of experience

These days, giving birth in the United States and other developed countries is extremely safe for mothers and babies. With good prenatal medical care and proper nutrition, the chances of a life-threatening emergency for mother or baby are exceedingly rare.

Occasionally, however, emergencies that require lightning-quick action on the part of medical staff do occur. In a high-quality hospital, medical center, or childbirth center, doctors, nurses, midwives, and anesthesiologists literally run to offer care to a mother and baby the moment a problem is identified.

Postpartum hemorrhage is an emergency that requires just this kind of fast action and expert treatment. When a woman experiences a postpartum hemorrhage, things go from good to bad very quickly. The woman gives birth and everything seems fine. Then, suddenly, it's not—she is bleeding uncontrollably.

Hemorrhaging presents hospital staff with a race against time to save her life. But, thanks to the many advances in maternal fetal medical care, and the dedication of skilled care providers, postpartum hemorrhages can almost always be stopped.

Terry's story serves as a good reminder that even when a pregnancy is apparently normal and low-risk, it's crucial to have a team of experts close by. Even the most routine delivery can sometimes quickly become an emergency.

The night I first met Terry was a stormy winter night and snow had been falling for several days. With freezing temperatures and 40 mph winds, it was not a night to be outside.

I was on duty at the hospital and at around 10 pm, I received a call from Dr. Johnson, a member of our staff. His patient, Mrs. Terry Clark, was in labor and she and her husband were en route to the hospital. Since I was already there, Dr. Johnson asked if I would care for his patient and I said I would be happy to.

Dr. Johnson gave me some background on Terry. She was pregnant with her third child, and her pregnancy had been entirely normal. Neither of us anticipated problems.

Terry, a pleasant thirty-two-year-old, was in active labor when she arrived at the hospital with her husband. My examination showed that everything was progressing normally, and I estimated she would probably deliver in two or three hours. I left her in the hands of our excellent nurses, who had already started intravenous fluids and placed a monitor on her to record uterine contractions and the baby's heart rate.

I went to see Terry again sometime later. She was already pushing with each contraction. Shortly thereafter, the infant's head was down in the pelvis and Terry's cervix was fully dilated. The baby's head began to show, becoming more visible with each contraction. Terry's perineum thinned out, and in a long and sustained push the head delivered spontaneously. The rest of the body followed and the baby, a boy, cried instantly.

I cut the cord and placed him on Terry's abdomen. Both Terry and her husband could not be any happier. The baby had instinctively grasped his mother's finger when she placed it on his palm, a tender reflex for the mother and a sign to me that the infant was reacting well to stimulation. The nurse cleaned and weighed him, then wrapped him in a blanket and returned him to his mother. Everything had progressed as expected.

The placenta followed shortly thereafter. I inspected it to make sure nothing was left behind and checked Terry for tears or abnormal bleeding. Everything seemed perfectly fine. When I finished, I left Terry and her husband and headed for another room, where another patient was in early labor.

About half an hour later, I was at the nursing station writing some notes when I heard nurse cry out. "Call Dr. Aladjem, STAT!" I turned around to see what the commotion was. The nurse assigned to Terry was running toward me. "Thank God you are still here! Terry is bleeding like you wouldn't believe!"

I rushed into the room. Terry's bed was covered with blood. I placed my hand on her abdomen. The uterus felt soft, instead of firm, and was well above the navel, which indicated it was not contracting as it should and was probably full of blood. Terry was having a postpartum hemorrhage.

There are very few obstetrical emergencies more frightening or more dangerous than a postpartum hemorrhage. It challenges the obstetrician's calmness, clear thinking, and experience more than almost anything else.

As I squeezed and compressed Terry's uterus, an explosive gush of blood came from the uterus. Blood spilled all over the bed and floor. I could see that Terry was frightened, so I told her not to worry, that she would be all right. Her husband was pale, too, so I suggested he sit in the waiting room while Terry was taken to the operating room for examination.

I ordered four units of blood and asked the blood bank to have a few more ready. I also asked an anesthesiologist to stand by in case Terry needed emergency surgery.

There are several possible causes for such a dramatic postpartum hemorrhage. The most common is a piece of the placenta left behind. I doubted this to be the case, because I had inspected it carefully and had found no evidence of missing pieces.

Sometimes, there is an additional small placenta connected to the main placenta, called a succenturiate lobe. This may be left behind while the expelled placenta appears intact. Usually, it is detected in an ultrasound performed during pregnancy, but Terry's chart gave no indication of an additional placenta.

Another possible cause is a tear in the birth canal. I had not seen one, but it was possible I had missed it during my after-delivery examination. Or the uterus may have ruptured during delivery, again an unlikely possibility.

The most likely cause was that the uterus had simply lost its ability to contract. We don't know why this happens.

133

In the operating room, Terry's blood pressure and pulse were normal, which was a positive thing because it indicated that her blood loss, which I estimated at about two pints, was not yet putting her in danger. During pregnancy, a woman's blood volume increases by up to 45%. Having all that extra blood protects her recover from the blood loss associated with delivery. It had certainly helped Terry so far. I asked the nurse to continue to check Terry's blood pressure and pulse every five minutes.

Before I started my examination, the anesthesiologist gave Terry some medication to help her feel more comfortable, and he started transfusing her.

The whole time, I was pressing my right hand on Terry's abdomen, holding the uterus to keep it contracted. As soon as I took my hand away, significant bleeding started again. I asked the nurse to take over clamping her hand down on the uterus so I could examine the birth canal.

The birth canal looked good—no sign of tears. The inside of her uterus felt normal, free of placental tissue or any signs of rupture. But the uterus was flaccid and lacked tone, which told me this was a case of the uterus not contracting—a condition we refer to as "uterine atony."

We administered some medication to firm up the uterus and help it regain its normal tone and ability to contract. Soon, the bleeding began to subside. Terry appeared to be improving. Her vital signs were normal and I thought we were out of the woods. In the waiting room, I updated and reassured her husband.

But within minutes, as I was changing out of my bloody scrubs, my beeper vibrated with an emergency call from labor and delivery. Assuming Terry was in trouble, I didn't even bother answering the call—I just started running.

Terry was bleeding again, and her uterus was soft. The medications had stopped working. I massaged her uterus for quite some time and while it became firm, her bleeding did not stop, although it appeared more moderate. The other two units of blood had arrived and we continued to transfuse her. I tried another drug, but it didn't solve the problem either.

I felt by now that our conservative efforts to stop Terry's bleeding had failed. If she continued to bleed, potentially dangerous complications could occur. It was time for surgery.

I would first attempt to tie the arteries that provide blood to the uterus. If that didn't work, I would have to perform a hysterectomy and remove her uterus. This is a decision of last resort, because without a uterus, Terry would be unable to have more children.

Once she was under anesthesia, I opened her abdomen and identified her uterine arteries on both sides of the uterus, placing sutures around them. Then I waited to see whether the uterus would contract and whether the bleeding would subside. I massaged the uterus for some time and placed warm towels on it.

A hush fell over the operating room while we waited to see whether the procedure had succeeded. I've seen this happen time and time again. Even though nobody on the hospital staff had met Terry before this night, they all cared deeply about her and her condition. I knew everyone in the room was silently hoping that the sutures would do the trick and a hysterectomy would not be necessary.

After about ten minutes, it looked like the bleeding had stopped. We all felt a sense of relief. The hustle and bustle of the operating room resumed. We closed Terry's abdomen and sent her to recovery.

The surgery was a complete success. A few days later, Terry and her husband brought home their healthy newborn son. Because of the blood loss and surgery, Terry was a bit more fatigued than she would have ordinarily been after giving birth. But before long, she would feel normal and her postpartum hemorrhage would be just a memory.

135

Thanks to fast action, excellent training, complete dedication, and years of experience, the hospital staff prevented a potential tragedy. Terry and her baby would both be perfectly fine.

* * *

I want him there!

Gone are the days when a husband was kept away from his laboring wife. Old movies show a doctor entering the house, asking for boiling water to be brought to the mother's bedside, and reassuring the husband, "She'll be OK," while disappearing into the bedroom. Then, all of a sudden, a baby's cry would ring out and the smiling doctor would appear, telling the husband "You have a boy" or "You have a girl."

When deliveries were first moved from the house to the hospital, fathers were relegated to "husbands' waiting rooms" during labor and delivery, where, together with other expectant fathers, they would drink coffee, smoke cigarettes, and exchange stories.

Today, prospective mothers tell friends "we are expecting" meaning both she and the baby's father. Together, they go to prenatal classes, take Lamaze classes, learn how to breathe and push, and the husband learns how to support the mother to be—physically, emotionally and verbally. Labor and delivery, in our culture, has become a family affair. Fathers are expected to be with the future mother throughout labor and delivery, and family members are usually welcome to be there too.

But it does not always work out that way.

Lisa and Glenn came to see me as soon as Lisa thought she might be pregnant. Lisa was in her early twenties and her husband was a couple of years older. This was her first pregnancy. They were both as excited as they could be, particularly since Lisa had experienced some problems getting pregnant which had required that she undergo fertility treatment. Now, they were looking forward to becoming parents for the first time.

Lisa's pregnancy appeared to progressing without incident. I had no reasons to expect any problems. Lisa wanted to know if she could participate in prenatal classes, and since she was planning to a have a "natural" birth, she also wanted to register for Lamaze classes. I told her that she most certainly could do that.

By the middle of the pregnancy, I received a call from Glenn. He wanted to know if he could come and talk to me alone. He reassured me that Lisa was doing well, but he needed to talk to me privately. He came to see me the following day and appeared quite troubled. He told me that he has been going with Lisa to prenatal and Lamaze classes, and he had a problem: he did not think he wanted to be with Lisa during labor and delivery. From what he had learned during those classes, the idea of being at the delivery did not appeal to him. He was worried about the sight of blood and the idea of seeing Lisa with labor pains was more than he could handle. Lisa was not receptive to the idea of him not being there. He asked whether I could please talk to Lisa.

We talked for a while about Glenn's concerns, and it became obvious to me that it probably would be better if he stayed away from the labor and delivery room. I told him I would be glad to talk to both of them at the same time, rather than talking to Lisa alone. He agreed and I asked him to accompany Lisa to her next appointment.

The following week, Lisa came to the office for her regular appointment. Glenn was not with her. This did not look good! Lisa was fine, but even before I had the opportunity to bring up the subject, Lisa told me she and Glenn had a problem. Glenn did not want to be present during her labor and delivery, and she wanted him there. Glenn had told her about him coming to talk to me the previous week, and they had apparently had quite an argument about that. Lisa seemed to not understand Glenn's position at all, and he was resolutely determined not to attend the labor and delivery.

Although I had seen other reluctant husbands, most eventually agree to be with their partner during labor and delivery. In this case, not only was Glenn unwilling to accompany Lisa, but she considered her husband's position as a sign of him "not loving her."

I asked Lisa why Glenn did not wish to accompany her, and she told me that he just did not want to come. My efforts to mediate their conflict did not go very far. Unsure whether the conflict was the result of deeper problems, I suggested they might want to consider seeing a counselor, which she immediately declined. I also told Lisa that her conclusion that Glenn does not love her was probably a wrong conclusion, and that some people were just not able to be present when medical procedures, in this case a delivery, take place. Surely, she should be able to understand that. She did not.

I explained to Lisa that I would be glad to talk to them together at any time, should they so desire. She thanked me and left.

At her next several appointments, Lisa did not raise the subject again. Her pregnancy progressed normally. A few weeks before delivery, she told me that she had been able to convince Glenn to accompany her, and she was pleased.

Lisa went into labor just a few days before her due date. When I arrived at the hospital, I found Lisa in early labor. Glenn was with her, and at one point told me: "I hope I'll make it."
"Be positive," I replied, "husbands do this all the time."

Lisa's labor progressed as expected. By late afternoon, her cervix was fully dilated and she started pushing. I was beginning to feel sorry for Glenn. He was obviously unable to be part of the process. He had to sit down several times, and as Lisa's pushing became more laborious he became quite pale. At one point, I suggested he exit the room, and have a cup of coffee. Lisa told him, "Come back soon or you'll miss everything."

Glenn left, and, frankly, I hoped he might stay out until Lisa delivered. But he came back after just a couple of minutes. The color had returned to his face and he went to his wife's side. Lisa was almost ready to deliver. She continued to push and the nurse was encouraging, coaching her.
"You OK?" the nurse asked Glenn. He nodded, indicating he was fine. Over the next ten minutes the baby's head came down and Lisa was pushing hard. With the last push, as the baby's head was rotating and coming out, Lisa let out an excruciating cry and the baby was delivered, followed by a gush of blood.

All we heard was a sudden thump. "He's out," the nurse said, instinctively pushing the emergency call button. Two nurses ran into the room.

"The father passed out," the attending nurse told the incoming nurses. "Take over."

The baby's cry added to the commotion and I placed the newborn, a healthy boy, on Lisa's abdomen.

Glenn seemed to recover without much delay. He was still pale and sweaty, and his blood pressure was low, as expected. A cursory exam showed that he had not injured himself in the fall. I asked the nurses to bring in a wheelchair and take Glenn to ER for a thorough examination.

"I am sorry," Lisa told us finally. "What exactly happened?"

"Glenn passed out," I told her. "He'll be OK. You have a beautiful baby boy.

"I am sorry," she said again.

"Don't worry, it's just another day in labor and delivery." I said smiling.

Kids having kids

Once upon a time, if you told someone that you were pregnant, you most likely were over twenty-one and married. Out-of-wedlock births were quite rare; when they happened, the social mores were such that they were considered a social stigma. It would have been unlikely that a woman told anyone about it, and most likely they would have gone out of town to deliver. In 1940, there were only about 89,000 out-of-wedlock births in the USA. By 1993, the yearly number of out-of-wedlock pregnancies rose to around 1.2 million.

Teenagers were certainly not immune to the sexual revolution that was happening around them in the mid-sixties. Books, movies, television programs, and popular music all glorified the acceptance and promotion of early sexual activity. Teenage pregnancies became almost an epidemic. In 2006, out of about 4 million births in the USA, 750,000 occurred in teenagers between the ages of fifteen and nineteen. Available data shows that the United States has one of the highest teenage pregnancy rates among industrialized nations: 53 per 1000 in women ages fifteen to nineteen. South Korea and Japan have the lowest rate, about one tenth that of the USA.

Teenage pregnancy has social, medical, and familial implications. Sometimes, it is very difficult to separate one from the other, since they intertwine very closely. Teenage pregnancy affects two families: that of the teenage mother and that of the teenage father. How their families react to the news depends on a multitude of factors. Shock is the common first reaction, followed by anger. It is not uncommon for the teenage father's family to distance themselves from that of the teenage mother. There are, of course, exceptions.

Probably one of the most difficult things for the parents of a pregnant teenage girl to accept is that their daughter was sexually active; being pregnant comes in second. For the teenage boy's family, the reverse seems true. While the boy's parents are rarely surprised their son was sexually active, the fact that he carelessly impregnated a young girl seems to be the focus of their initial anger.

During my professional career, I have had the opportunity to take care of many teenage mothers. The story of Bridget is one of compassion, understanding and love, but not without challenges.

Bridget, a fifteen-year-old girl, was referred to me by her pediatrician. Given Bridget's age, she automatically fell into the high-risk patient category. When I walked into the consulting room to meet Bridget, I felt like I was facing a congregation! In addition to Bridget, there were her parents, the teenage father-to-be, and his parents. The presence of both sets of parents was encouraging, as I assumed these kids probably had their parents' support.

Bridget was a tiny girl for her age, appearing to be little older than twelve or thirteen. She was sitting between her mother and her father, with her head down and her face flushed. Her boyfriend was standing behind his parents. He was tall, probably five-foot-eight or so, neatly dressed and wearing his high school jacket. I guessed Bridget's parents to be in their late thirties while the boy's parents were probably mid-forties.

I introduced myself to them and Bridget's father replied first, introducing himself and everybody else. Her boyfriend's name was Benjamin and he was seventeen years old. Bridget's father continued by saying that while this was not the best thing that could have happened, he wanted me to know that he and his wife, as well as Benjamin's parents, were supportive of their kids. I thanked him and told them I was glad to hear that.

It was no surprise to hear that this was an unplanned pregnancy. Bridget was unsure how many weeks pregnant she might be. Her periods were irregular and she did not know when she might have become pregnant. At that point in time, I thought we needed to have some privacy. I suggested that Bridget and her mother accompany me to an examining room and told the rest of the family we would return in about thirty minutes. They were welcome to stay in the conference room, or to leave and come back later. They chose to wait there.

From her pediatrician's note, I knew Bridget was in good general health. She was fifteen years and three months old. Her mother confirmed that Bridget's first menstrual period had been at age thirteen, but that she was always irregular. Sometimes, two to three months would pass without a period. At her age, that was not unusual. Menstrual periods in a young girl may not be accompanied by ovulation at first, in the medical name for which is "anovulatory bleeding." As a result, bleeding does not follow a pattern as it does in adult women. In Bridget's case, bleeding episodes had become more regular and the interval between them was shortening. Bridget became sexually active after her fourteenth birthday.

The rest of her medical history was unremarkable. She was doing well in school. Both of her parents were healthy, and there was nothing unusual in her family history. To the best of their knowledge, Benjamin's family was also healthy.

I told Bridget that I would ask the nurse to come in and help her undress so that I could examine her. Her physical examination was entirely normal. An ultrasound confirmed that Bridget was about twenty-six weeks pregnant. Before returning to the conference room, I asked if they wanted to have information about Bridget's care shared with Benjamin and his family. I explained that confidentiality is important and that I would follow their wishes. Bridget's mother told me that she was happy to let them know, which was fine with me.

We returned to the conference room where everybody was waiting. Bridget's mother informed everybody that the pregnancy was twenty-six and a half weeks along, and that Bridget was doing well. For my part, I told Bridget I wanted to see her in two weeks. The nurse gave Bridget a laboratory order for her to complete all the needed prenatal laboratory work before her next visit. I told them to call me at any time if needed, and that I expected to see Bridget in two weeks.

I must confess that I feel very deeply for any family confronted with a teenage pregnancy. Kids having kids is an occurrence that would disrupt any family. When the parents, after their initial shock, decide to be supportive, it lessens the burden on the kids, but the situation will always remain worrisome to the parents. There are always mixed emotions, occasionally guilt—"Where did we go wrong?"—and certainly a struggle to accept that their baby is going to have a child of her own. In circumstances were the parents are not supportive, or the teenagers decide not to tell their parents, mistakes may be made that might lead to disaster. I was pleased that Bridget's and Benjamin's parents were supportive.

During the next two months, Bridget continued to see me regularly and over that time I got to know her better. She told me how her pregnancy had changed her, how difficult it had been to tell her parents, how her parents had reacted to the news, and how thankful she was that they were supportive of her.
"I understand my parents better now, and I could not have gone through this without them," she said one day. She had certainly came a long way from being the shy girl I had met at her first visit, sitting between her parents, hanging her head.
I asked her how Benjamin was taking all this. "He is not ready to be a father," she told me. "But he's OK."
I asked her why.
"Things, just things," she said.
I did not ask any more questions; I thought, however, about how a girl can mature into a young woman in such a short time.

At her thirty-four-week appointment, I noticed Bridget had increased in weight significantly in just one week. Her extremities were swollen, her blood pressure was mildly elevated, and her reflexes were brisk. She was showing symptoms of early preeclampsia. Preeclampsia in young mothers is quite common, and is not to be taken lightly. I decided to hospitalize her.

Shortly after she was admitted to hospital, I started her on magnesium sulphate, a medication commonly used in preeclampsiaas. This medication prevents maternal seizures, a complication of preeclampsia that is known as eclampsia.

In the following twelve hours, Bridget's laboratory values took a turn for the worst and indicated that a clotting disorder was developing—a dangerous complication of preeclampsia. It was time to deliver her as soon as possible.

An induction of labor was started and soon after, Bridget was in labor. I told her parents they should be prepared for a long night. I wondered why neither Benjamin nor his parents were there, but then remembered Bridget telling me that Benjamin was not ready to be a father. I decided it was not my place to ask.

By midnight, we had some signs of potential new problems. The infant's heartbeat was slowing with each contraction, a sign that the infant was under stress and was not tolerating labor. This was the result of the uterine contractions, which decrease blood flow to the placenta and consequently make less oxygen available to the baby. We placed an oxygen mask on Bridget in order to increase the amount of oxygen going to the infant. I also asked the nurse to call blood bank and have two units of blood available for Bridget in case we needed to perform an emergency cesarean section.

I explained to Bridget and her parents why the baby's heart was slowing down, and why she was wearing an oxygen mask. I also indicated that unless these episodes improved, we might have to deliver the baby by cesarean section.

The next couple of hours proceeded without major incident. Bridget was in good labor and the infant's heart beat had stopped slowing down. I returned to see her around midnight. The labor room was quiet, with only two other patients in labor that night. Bridget's mother was by her side, talking softly, and her father was in an armchair dozing. He stood up when I walked in and asked, "How's she doing?"
"She is stable," I said. I had barely finished speaking, when a prolonged and intense contraction occurred and remained at its peak for a good forty-five seconds. Bridget began complaining

immediately, "Oh God, my tummy, my tummy…" At the same time, the baby's heart dropped precipitously from a normal 120 beats per minute to below 80, and stayed there. Instinctively, I uncovered Bridget and saw a pool of blood between her legs. "She's abrupting," I told the nurse, meaning that the placenta was separating from the uterus prematurely. "Call anesthesia and blood bank and let's move to the operating room—NOW!" Two other nurses ran into the room, and as fast as one can imagine, Bridget was on her way to the operating room. I told the parents, "Come with me." On the way to the operating room, I explained what was happening as fast as I could and told them we would have to do an emergency cesarean section. "She'll be OK," I reassured them. By that time, the anesthesiologist had arrived, so I updated him on the situation.

"Ok," he said. "Let's go."

I scrubbed as fast as I could. When I entered the operating room, Bridget was already on the operating table. The scrub nurse was counting and setting the instruments on her table, while the circulating nurse, after removing the monitors, was pouring iodine onto Bridget's abdomen. "She's ready," she told me, as I put on my gown and gloves. The anesthesiologist was instructing Bridget to breathe deeply, which meant she was going to sleep. With the assistance of the scrub nurse, I draped Bridget abdomen. "Whenever you are ready," the anesthesiologist told me. "She's asleep and doing well."

I made a fast incision and opened her abdomen. Her uterus appeared bluish in some areas, a sign of significant blood loss, and that blood had infiltrated the uterine muscle. When I opened the uterus, a gush of blood emerged. I grabbed the infant by its head and lifted it out of its mother's uterus. It was a boy. The scrub nurse clamped the cord, cut it, and handed the baby to the attending neonatology nurse. From the moment we started rushing towards the operating room, to the birth of the baby, not more than ten minutes had elapsed. The neonatologist took over the care of the newborn while I removed the placenta. It quickly became clear that about half of it had separated. There was a big clot on its surface. I cleared the uterus of remaining blood and clots, and squeezed the uterus to force it to contract.

We heard the baby cry. A wonderful cry, thank God!
The anesthesiologist asked me my estimation of Bridget's blood loss. "At least two units," I said. The blood had arrived into the operating room, so he started infusing the blood. "Bridget is just fine," he told me.

I closed the uterus, pleased to see it was firm and contracting well. I then removed any blood clots from the abdominal cavity and proceeded to close the abdomen. After finishing the surgery, I went to see Bridget's parents in the waiting room. I gave them a detailed explanation of what happened, since I was sure that they must have been frightened by the sudden and unexpected sequence of events. I reassured them that Bridget was OK, and that she had a baby boy. They could see their daughter in the recovery room in a few minutes.
"Is the baby, OK?" her father asked.
"He cried immediately after his birth," I said. Then I added that the neonatologist would come to speak to them as soon as he finished examining the infant.

While I was talking to them, the neonatologist entered the room. He introduced himself and told them baby was healthy and he had tolerated the ordeal well. When I went to see Bridget, she was holding her newborn. She smiled at me and said, "Isn't he beautiful? It's my baby."
I asked her how she was feeling, and she nodded, implying she was doing well. Her eyes were filled with tears.
"Would you like to know more about what happened to you?" I asked her.
"I know," she said. "I just had a baby, and you helped. Thank you."
I was speechless. It was amazing how fast one girl can grow up. She was not a fifteen-year-old girl anymore; she was a mother!

* * *

Where's the baby?

Imagination is a wonderful thing. Close your eyes, and you are instantly transported into a world of fantasy, limited only by your own creativity. Open your eyes, and you are back in your living room, at your desk, on the plane, or wherever you were in reality. Such daydreaming is perfectly normal. Sometimes, however, the mind takes over and makes the body actually believe that what a person is imagining is the truth. That, of course, is not normal.

Sometimes, a woman's desire to get pregnant is so powerful that she imagines she *is* pregnant. Her mind takes over, and her body even believes that it is pregnant. Hormonal changes occur, menstrual periods stop, morning sickness appears, breasts become engorged, the abdomen feels full and may even enlarge, and weight is gained. Everything points to a pregnancy, except for the fact that there is no pregnancy. This phenomenon is known as "pseudocyesis," or "false pregnancy." It is very rare, but it does happen. Historically, the most famous woman who believed she was pregnant but was not was Mary Tudor, Queen of England, in the sixteenth century.

My patient, Edith, was admitted to the hospital emergency room with abdominal pains, which she interpreted as being in labor. She had not undergone any prenatal care; therefore, she never saw a doctor throughout her pregnancy. Under the circumstances, Edith became a high-risk patient. I was on call for our service, so the ER physician called to let me know Edith was on her way to the labor and delivery area. In turn, I called the labor and delivery nursing desk to let them know she was coming, and to tell them I would be there shortly.

Edith was being wheeled in as I arrived. Not knowing what to expect, I told the nurse I would talk to her first. Edith was thirty-eight years old and this was her second pregnancy. Her first pregnancy had been at age seventeen. Circumstances were such that she had placed her baby boy up for adoption. Edith had never seen him again, nor did she know who had adopted him. She was a waitress in a local restaurant, was unmarried, and lived with her mother. While she had a boyfriend, he was "not involved."

Edith's story, unfortunately, was not new to me. With minor variations, I had heard it many times over. She appeared to be healthy and neat in appearance, and I asked her why she had not sought prenatal care. She told me that at first she did not realize she was pregnant, and that it was only when she had missed a couple of periods that the thought of being pregnant came to mind. Unfortunately, she had no insurance at work, and she did not qualify for Medicaid. Figuring she was healthy, she had hoped for the best. Edith did not know for sure when she was due, but going by the date of her last menstrual period, we figured she should be due any day now.

It struck me as unusual that during our conversation she had not complained once about labor pains. I told her that the ER physician had said she was in labor and asked whether she felt any contractions at all. She told me that it was not too bad as they seemed to have slowed down.

I asked the nurse, Janine, to admit Edith, and told her I would examine her shortly. I also asked Janine to put a monitor on her. Before leaving the room, I let Janine know I would be in the record room, signing some old charts that I had pending there, and would return. Should she need me, I instructed she should page me.

I had been in the record room for about ten minutes before my beeper started flashing. I doubted very much that Edith was suddenly ready to deliver. In fact, my first impression was that she was probably not in labor at all, and that it may have been a false alarm. But things happen in obstetrics without warning, so I called labor and delivery immediately. Janine told me that she could not localize the baby's heart beating, nor could she pick any contractions on the monitor. "Maybe it's because she is kind of heavy, but I am concerned," she told me. I had worked with Janine for many years, and if she was concerned, I was too. I told her I was on my way.

149

My mind was in overdrive. Could the baby have died? But why? Maybe that was why the contractions had suddenly stopped. It is not unusual for that to happen when a baby dies early in labor. *There we are*, I thought to myself, *the price of no prenatal care, again. Damn!*

As I was wondering what on earth was going on, instinctively my walking pace increased. I hurried directly to Edith's room. Janine was still trying to locate the baby's heart by moving the transducer back and forth on Edith's abdomen. She stopped when she saw me enter the room. Edith was indeed on the heavy side. I noted, strangely, that the skin of her abdomen did not show a single stretch mark. That was unusual for someone who had already had one pregnancy and who was supposed to be at term. I put both of my hands on Edith's abdomen, trying to palpate the uterus and stimulate the baby into moving. Janine was watching me inquisitively. I could palpate the abdomen very easily, but I could not feel the uterus or the baby.

"What's going on?" Edith asked.
"Don't know yet," I told her. "Was the baby active today?"
"Of course," Edith said. "It is a very active baby. What's wrong with my baby?"
Still not knowing what I was dealing with, while waiting for Janine to bring in the portable ultrasound equipment, my mind was running through the possibilities. Edith definitely did not have a term pregnancy—my inability to palpate the uterus and the baby clearly told me that. Conceivably, the baby may have died sometime during pregnancy. Since Edith never saw a physician during her pregnancy, she would not have known that. Sometimes, infants die before birth and may be retained for long periods of time without the mother going into labor. The danger to the mother, in such situations, is that the death of the fetus may eventually alter the mother's blood clotting system, a condition known as DIC, or disseminated intravascular coagulation. This condition may evolve over weeks or months and has the potential to threaten the mother's life. Soon after the death of the baby, the perceived movements by the mother are nothing but the result of the infant being displaced

by maternal movements. The mother feels the displacement and thinks the baby is moving.

Janine brought the ultrasound equipment. Edith immediately asked if she could see the baby. I told her that once I completed the ultrasound study, I would show her. I placed the equipment near Edith's bed, with the screen visible to me. I had to know what I was dealing with before showing the image to Edith. I started scanning in the middle of the abdomen. From there, I was able to systematically scan in all directions. I kept scanning in stunned disbelief. Edith had a perfectly normal abdomen, without any signs of pregnancy. What I was dealing with was a false pregnancy.

How was I going to break the news to Edith? This was no minor problem. False pregnancies happen sometimes in patients who have serious psychiatric problems, such as in schizophrenics. I was no psychiatrist, but during my interaction with Edith, I had found her to be very down-to-earth and never had the feeling she was suffering from a mental illness. Certainly, anyone with a false pregnancy may potentially have some psychological problems, which is different than having a mental illness. I quickly decided to follow my instinct. If she were a schizophrenic with a delusion of pregnancy, we would have to deal with that later.

All this time, Janine was behind my back, staring at the screen. She did not say a word, but I knew what she was thinking. Edith was the first to speak. "Can I see the baby now?" I turned the ultrasound machine towards her. She looked at the screen and asked, "Where's the baby?" In the calmest voice I could muster, I said, "Edith, there is no baby. You are not pregnant. Let's talk about it." Edith looked at the screen, and then looked at me and Janine. Her eyes filled with tears and she started sobbing. "What do you mean there is no baby? I had no periods, my breasts hurt, I was cramping just like labor when I came in." I scanned her abdomen again and showed her the content of her abdomen, bowels, uterus, and ovaries. "See, there is no baby, Edith. You thought you were pregnant, and because of that, your body reacted like you were pregnant. Rarely, women can do that. It's called false pregnancy." Edith was crying but was not fighting the reality, which reassured me she had no mental illness.

I felt sorry for her. The little I knew about her was enough for me to see that her life may have been a fertile ground for a false pregnancy. At seventeen, she had given up her first child for adoption and over time she had probably had various personal relations. She was of "advanced age" by obstetrical standards, and she was living with her mother. Her current boyfriend "was not involved." The mind can play dirty tricks in such circumstances.

I told Edith I was willing to listen if she wanted to talk about it now. Appearing more composed, she said that she would, but a little bit later. I asked her to let Janine know when she felt like talking to me and I would return.

Word spread like wildfire among the labor and delivery staff. Nobody had ever seen a false pregnancy before. I told everyone, in no uncertain terms, that they were to interact with Edith exactly the same as they would with any other patient. No personal questions, no whispering behind her back—just normal, routine activity!

About an hour or so later, Janine called to tell me that Edith would like to go home but would first like to talk to me. I returned to Edith's room. Considering the situation, I thought she was handling admirably.

Her first question was: "How could I fool myself like that and for such a long time?" Her voice was firm, but it was obvious she was fighting back tears. That she was not denying the reality of the situation was an excellent sign, under the circumstances. I started by explaining to Edith what a false pregnancy was all about. As we went along, I answered her many questions.

She told me that all her life she had wanted a child, but that she was never in very stable relationships, so had avoided getting pregnant. She had not been thinking of getting pregnant, when she had suddenly missed a period, and then another one. That's when she thought she might be pregnant. "I guess I talked myself into it, as you say," she said. But she could not believe that her breasts had become engorged or that she had gained weight. And she wondered how I could explain that she had felt what appeared to be the baby moving?

It was not easy to explain. Some people think that abdominal gas might be mistaken for fetal movements; others believe that the psychological impact of a false pregnancy is so great, that the mind really imagines feeling the baby move. Edith told me that she could not decide right then whether to feel relieved or if depressed. I suggested that she needed to resolve some psychological problems. Since she had no insurance, I could arrange, through our social worker, to have her seen by a counselor at a center that accepted uninsured patients in need. She agreed.

By that time, it was quite late in the evening. I suggested she stay overnight and that, in the morning, I would ask the social worker to make arrangements for her to see a counselor. Furthermore, I asked if she had someone who could come in and drive her home. She told me her mother could come. I did not say it, but I did not think she should leave the hospital unaccompanied. I felt it was safer that way.

Several weeks later, I received a letter from the psychologist who had been taking care of Edith. She was showing amazing progress in dealing with those factors in her life that had led to her imaginary pregnancy.

* * *

My twin brother is weeks younger than me

Is it possible for twins to have different birthdays, weeks apart from each other? Yes, it is!

This is the story of Arlene and her twins. Arlene could not have been happier when her doctor, a family physician, told her she was carrying twins. This was her first pregnancy and she was referred to a maternal fetal medicine specialist because, twins, triplets or any other multiples, are always considered high risk.

When I entered the examining room at Arlene's first visit, she and her husband Frank were holding hands. Many years of practicing high-risk obstetrics instinctively told me they were a couple that would "be there" for each other. But right now, they both were clearly experiencing a high degree of anxiety and apprehension. Arlene's hands were trembling, and I understood their fears and anxieties. They were being referred to a specialist in high-risk pregnancies. What was wrong?

I introduced myself and began to explain why they had been referred to me. "Twin pregnancies are considered high risk since certain complications are more likely to occur when compared to a single pregnancy," I started to tell them. "With twins, there is a greater chance of premature delivery. The human uterus is designed to carry one fetus, so more than one puts the pregnancy at risk. The uterus increases in size at a faster rate with multiples, and that may trigger early labor. The mother also has more of a chance of developing high blood pressure and preeclampsia. Why this happens, we don't really know, but it does. At the time of labor, one or both of the twins may not be in a position that will allow a vaginal delivery, and therefore, cesarean sections are more likely to be needed. Your doctor sent me a note about you, and I am glad to see that you are a very healthy young lady," I said.

"I never had any health problems before," Arlene said. "What concerns me is why I was referred here. What's wrong with my pregnancy? Are the babies going to be all right? Is there something wrong already?"

"Your doctor is a family physician, not an obstetrician, and he probably felt that since twin pregnancies sometimes have problems, transferring your care while everything was well would be better than an emergency transfer later. I call this good medicine." I could sense that their apprehension was beginning to diminish.

"I see," Arlene hesitated for a moment and then asked, "In my case, what potential problems should I be concerned about?"

"We'll talk about that, but if you don't mind, let me first complete your history and perform an ultrasound and an examination. Then we can talk and I will answer any questions you may have."

During the ultrasound examination, I spent some extra time showing them the two infants. Visualization of the infant during an ultrasound examination is always very reassuring to parents. In this particular case, they were able to see both hearts beating and both babies moving. Showing them the baby's faces, their bodies, and taking the first pictures of their babies, had a soothing effect upon Arlene and Frank, which was good. Arlene was about nineteen weeks pregnant and all seemed well. I asked if they wanted to know the sex of their babies, and both said they did. One was a boy, and the other a girl. Arlene started crying and Frank kissed her. They were happy.

After the ultrasound and the examination that followed, we met in my office to discuss my assessment and to answer their questions.

"You are nineteen weeks pregnant," I told her, "and I cannot find any problems that would concern me at this time." I reassured them that the majority of twin pregnancies proceed without problems. I answered their questions and then asked her to schedule an appointment in two weeks time for a routine checkup, as I prefer to see patients who are carrying twins every two weeks, rather than monthly, which is standard for single pregnancies.

Arlene's pregnancy continued satisfactorily and follow-up ultrasound examinations showed the babies were developing according to what we would expect for twins. By the time Arlene reached twenty-six weeks however, the ultrasound scan showed some changes in cervix length and shape—signs that concerned me. That early in pregnancy, such changes usually indicated the threat of preterm labor. I asked Arlene if she had felt any contractions.

"No" she replied, "I have not."

I shared the ultrasound results with Arlene and asked her to stay off her feet as much as possible, to report any contractions immediately, and to avoid sexual activity, since that might stimulate uterine contractions. I asked her to return in four days. Four days later, the ultrasound showed her cervix had shortened even more; plus, it was not as tightly closed as it should be. Arlene was still not feeling any contractions, but I decided to hospitalize her just in case.

Once in the hospital, the nurse placed a monitoring device on Arlene's abdomen in order to record any contractions she might have, and both babies' heartbeats, which would allow us to assess the infants' well-being.

It became apparent that Arlene's uterus was contracting, even if she could not feel the contractions and had no discomfort. It was a situation we call an irritable uterus. While such contractions are not strong enough to be felt, they are nonetheless strong enough to produce changes in the cervix over time. Left unchecked, they eventually become stronger and premature labor ensues. In such cases, we use intravenous medication in an attempt to slow down the irritability of the uterus. If we are successful, we can eventually start oral medication to keep the uterus quiet and to stop contractions.

I explained to Arlene and Frank what was happening, and what we were doing. I also told her she had to be prepared for a long stay in hospital, She was not yet twenty-seven weeks pregnant. and as the possibility existed that we might fail in our attempt to control premature labor, we had to start preparing for the possibility of delivering premature twins.

There is nothing more frightening to expectant parents than not knowing what may happen and what to expect. Should a crisis occur, that is not the time one to assume parents understand what is taking place; therefore, I told them I would arrange a meeting with our neonatologists, who specialize in the care of newborns. A newborn is not a "small" infant. The transition from life before birth to life after birth is a very delicate path that the infant has to cross. Critically, when a baby is born prematurely, not all of its organs are ready to function normally. The lungs, in particular, may be immature and unable to perform their vital function of breathing. That along might be the difference between a premature baby's survival and death. Neonatal care, therefore, often means critical care and life support, and neonatologists are trained to do just that.

I encourage parents to visit the Neonatal Intensive Care Unit (NICU) to see for themselves what is going on there, long before their own child might have to be admitted. When one is not emotionally involved, we are always better able to absorb information, and, as they say, knowledge is power. Nowhere is that saying more true than when a parent has to watch his or her infant fighting for its life.

We had a joint meeting with the neonatologists who were to care for the twins once they were born. They explained to Arlene and Frank what to expect if delivery were to occur so early in pregnancy. While Arlene was at a stage where infants had a good chance of survival, there was still always the potential for serious problems with the newborn. In anticipation of an early delivery, we treated Arlene with corticosteroids, a drug that would accelerate the lung maturity of her infants. Respiratory problems are common in premature infants of such an early gestational age.

For three days, we continued to control Arlene's contractions, which by now, she could feel. Her cervix was opening and it became apparent we would not be able to stop her premature labor. The next morning, I got a call from a labor and delivery nurse, telling me Arlene was in full-blown labor.

157

I rushed to the hospital. Our efforts to stop her labor had failed, and we were preparing for an early delivery of twins. Sometime later that morning, she delivered, vaginally, the first of the twins: the baby girl. She weighed just one pound six ounces, but that was still quite a good weight for a twin of her gestational age. The neonatologist team was there and took care of the little girl, moving her to the neonatal intensive care unit. The neonatologist in charge told Arlene that the girl had some difficulties breathing, but that otherwise she appeared normal. He was cautiously optimistic about her having a good outcome.

After the birth of the girl, Arlene's contractions slowed down significantly. Labor slowing down after the delivery of the first twin was not uncommon. The cord of the first twin had been cut short, and I fully expected that labor would resume and the second twin would be born. Arlene was comfortable and was lovingly supported by Frank. We waited in the delivery room for the second twin to arrive. The neonatologist asked, "Well, Dr. Aladjem, is there another baby coming or not?"
"Be patient," I told him.

After about an hour, I decided to perform an ultrasound to take a look at the second baby. The baby boy had changed position from a "head first" or vertex position, to having repositioned himself across the uterine cavity—what we call a transverse lie. Infants in transverse lie cannot be delivered vaginally, and must be delivered by cesarean section.

The infant appeared, nevertheless, to be unaffected. The membranes of the second twin were intact and Arlene's cervix had now retracted from the full dilation that allowed the delivery of the first twin, to an almost closed conformation. Things were quiet! I did not feel any urgency to intervene. I left Arlene's room and told her I would return shortly.

I had some decisions to make. The short road would have been to perform a cesarean section and deliver the boy. I could not induce labor because of the infant's position. However, in pregnancies as premature as Arlene's, delayed delivery of the second twin is a viable alternative. I was concerned about the possibility of infection, but with the membranes of the second twin remaining intact, and the addition of antibiotics to Arlene's intravenous fluids, I could minimize or avoid that risk. Delaying delivery of the second twin would allow for the baby boy's lungs to mature, and he would hopefully avoid breathing problems after birth. Should labor restart at any time and the infant continued to be in transverse position, I would have to perform a cesarean section.

I needed to talk to Arlene and Frank to see how they felt about all this. It is of paramount importance for the mother to fully understand the plans, the risks, and the benefits. I could provide my best advice, but the patient has to understand and agree with my plan of management.

I went back to Arlene's room. She was comfortable.
"Is he ever going to be born?" she asked.
"Absolutely! The question is: when?" I proceeded to outline my assessment and plan to both of them, explaining that there was no immediate need for intervention and that a delay in the delivery of the boy might be beneficial. Such a decision was not without risks, however. We talked about the alternative—an immediate delivery by cesarean section because of the position of the infant—and about the risks and benefits of waiting for spontaneous labor to restart.

"How long can we go on like that?" Frank asked.
"That I cannot predict," I answered. "Anywhere from a few days to a few weeks, sometimes longer. I believe the longest reported case was slightly over three months."
I asked them if they would like to be alone to talk in private. "No, thank you," Arlene said. "We can all talk together, and if we have a question, you can answer it."
After a few questions and exchanges of thoughts between husband and wife, Arlene said, "I guess I will have to be pregnant a little while longer. Let's wait."
Frank agreed and asked, "Will she have to stay in the hospital?"
"Without question," I answered.

The monitoring of the second infant was reassuring. There were no signs of any problem, but I told them I would be in the hospital at least until the following morning, just in case. They thanked me. I decided to keep Arlene in the labor and delivery unit under constant monitoring.

The night was quiet. In the morning, I went to see how the little girl was doing, and was happy to discover she was holding her own. The neonatologist was optimistic, telling me that while she still needed help breathing, she was OK. He thought she would probably be able to breathe on her own shortly, and she had no other problems.

I went to see Arlene, who was well rested and having breakfast. She had no contractions and slept all night. Frank had gone home. I told her about her girl and also that one of the nurses would take her in a wheelchair to see the baby. She was overjoyed.

The following few days were uneventful. No signs of infection. No signs of labor. The baby boy was happy. I decided there was no need for her to continue to stay in the labor and delivery area, and we transferred her to the obstetrical unit.

Because of the infant lying across the uterine cavity, and fearing a possible sudden rupture of membranes that could drag the cord down into the vagina—a dangerous complication—I limited Arlene's movements. Frank was there morning and evening, and they were adjusting admirably under the circumstances.

As days passed, Arlene became the favorite patient on the obstetrical unit. Upon arrival of every new nursing shift, the first question was, "Is Arlene still undelivered?"
It became routine that just about everyone, from nurses to clerks, would stop by to say good morning, or good afternoon to Arlene.

Every day, I performed an ultrasound to see if the baby had changed position and to determine whether there were any changes in the cervix or in the amount of amniotic fluid. Everything was looking good. The fluid level was normal, which confirmed that the membranes were intact and that the amniotic fluid was not leaking. The cervix had closed; therefore, the risks of the cord being dragged down if the membranes were to rupture suddenly, were minimal. I told Arlene that she could walk around the corridor if she felt like, but that she should not leave the obstetrical unit.

I was pleased with her progress and with the decision to continue the pregnancy. Arlene reached thirty-two weeks, and one morning, my ultrasound showed that the infant had turned around and was now head down. It also appeared that the baby's head was coming down into her pelvis. The baby was getting ready for delivery. We estimated that the boy's weight was over three pounds, twice as big as his sister, who had been born a few weeks ago.

I shared my findings with Arlene, who asked if I was going to induce her labor. I told her that unless I had a reason to do so, which I did not at that time, I would not. I also told her that my impression was that she would start labor spontaneously very soon. The reason I thought labor would start sooner rather than later, was the low position of the infant's head up against the cervix, which was now thinned when compared to prior ultrasounds.

Over the next forty-eight hours, Arlene started experiencing contractions, but not enough to call it labor. By the third day, however, she was in labor. Shortly afterward, she vaginally delivered a healthy boy—three pounds, six ounces—who cried immediately and had no need for respiratory support.

Arlene had an uneventful postpartum course and three days after the boy's birth, she was ready to go home. The neonatologist felt that while the boy could probably go home in the near future, the girl, who by now was breathing on her own and was being fed without any problems, would need to stay in NICU for a while longer.

Both Arlene and Frank were delighted. It was not an easy time for either of them, but the thought of having two healthy babies compensated for the days of anguish that had endured.

Success stories like this make the art of practicing high-risk obstetrics a joy. Pregnancy can be a constant wonder, a reminder of how miraculous nature really can be.

* * *

Different cultures, different labors

Labor and delivery is the biological culmination of nine months of intrauterine growth and development. When the intrauterine life is unable to be prolonged any further, the time for the child to be born has arrived.

The process of childbirth is the same, no matter who you are, or where you are. However, from prehistoric times, this process has evolved social and cultural dimensions that differ across cultures. As such, the behavioral response to birthing could not be more different, depending on whether you are North American, South American, European, Chinese, or another nationality. These variations also depend upon the relevant subculture, or even the region in which the parents live, or the health concerns of the parent. It is true, for example, that diabetics health issues are the same whether they are American, Japanese, French or any other nationality. However, the perception of labor and delivery depends entirely upon the parents' social and cultural environment. No matter what a person's educational level is, the distinction between fact and fiction regarding labor and delivery can become blurred.

I have always been intrigued by how women's response to the discomfort of labor contractions can differ. Pain is pain, but the response to labor pain is modified by, controlled by, and really orchestrated by the patient's cultural and social background. I have witnessed an array of reactions to labor, from the subdued Asian woman, for whom vocalizing the discomfort is shameful and a sign of weakness, to the very loud Latina, who is expected to be vocal. How the pain is perceived and managed by the patient depends solely upon their mindset, which is modified by their culture.

Furthermore, family members play a role predetermined by tradition. Whether the mother or the mother-in-law will accompany the pregnant patient depends on where the mother-to-be is from. In Asian families, the mother-in-law usually attends the labor of her daughter-in-law. South American patients usually have their own mother at the birth. In many Asian cultures, the father does not get involved in the delivery process, but in parts of South America, the father may be a real participant in his wife's labor.

The afterbirth, or placenta, usually discarded in western cultures, is revered in others and is considered to contain the soul of the newborn; it may even be buried or be eaten. Some traditions have a rational explanation for popular beliefs. For example, Chinese prohibition of intercourse during pregnancy is surely based upon the observation that intercourse is sometimes followed by a miscarriage. Other traditions do not seem to have an apparent rational basis and may be more superstitious or based on empirical evidence. For example, women of the Yucatan Peninsula, Mexico, labor and deliver in a matrimonial hammock that was received as a wedding gift. In certain Mayan communities, those who attend the birth talk constantly talk to distract the mother-to-be's attention away from the pain and discomfort. For some South American Indians, delivery is considered such a normal event that labor and delivery occurs in public, where everybody can see it. The history of labor and delivery in various cultures is a telling story of man's evolution, and literature is rich on the subject.

What follows are the stories of a Chinese woman and two South American women in labor. All of these women taught me a lot about what birth is all about. Mrs. Lee was from Taiwan but living in the United States. Blanca was from Brazil and had been visiting her sister in Chicago when went into labor a few weeks before her due date. Consuelo originated from Peru and was temporarily living in the United States.

Mrs. Lee

Mrs. Lee and her husband came to my office at the suggestion of their family physician, Dr. Kim, who was also Taiwanese. The reason for the referral was that Mrs. Lee had lost two prior pregnancies for no apparent reason. Dr. Kim thought my evaluation and subsequent care might help her carry her existing pregnancy to term.

Mrs. Lee was thirty-two years old and very quiet, deferring to her husband in mostly everything. Mr. Lee was a professor at one of the colleges in the Chicago area. He was courteous, spoke good English, and was extremely polite. It soon became apparent that I would have to adapt my manner a little to be successful in my interaction with them. I asked them how long they had been in the United States, and Mr. Lee told me that he had arrived to go to college some twenty years ago and had met Mrs. Lee during his college years. Mrs. Lee had lived in the United States since childhood. Both were committed to keeping their cultural traditions intact, which I felt was important to keep in mind.

Mrs. Lee was presumed to be no more than six weeks pregnant, and I asked her to tell me exactly what had happened during her previous pregnancies. Unfortunately, as it is often the case, there was nothing unusual that she could tell me. She became pregnant, and miscarried both times around the second month of pregnancy. Nothing in her medical history explained her miscarriages. Now, about a year after her last miscarriage, she had become pregnant again and her physician had referred her to my office.

Her medical history was unremarkable. Mr. Lee was about ten years older and his history was also unremarkable. I suggested we perform an ultrasound to confirm the pregnancy, to which they agreed. The ultrasound confirmed she was pregnant and at six to seven weeks gestation. It also told me that her uterus appeared entirely normal, which was reassuring, since abnormality in the shape of the uterus can go undetected and could be a cause of miscarriage. Mrs. Lee's physical examination was also entirely normal. I decided to perform a series of laboratory blood tests to rule out any systemic problem. I explained to them that her history was not that out of the ordinary. Many women have early miscarriages without us being able to find a specific cause. I asked them to see me again in two weeks, at which time we would discuss the laboratory results and establish a care plan for her. I encouraged them to call me at any time should there be any problems or should they have any questions. I also told them that, should the laboratory test show anything troublesome, I would give them a call before their next visit. They thanked me profusely and left.

I was not surprised when all of Mrs. Lee's laboratory blood tests were reported as normal. We are rarely able to determine the specific cause of early pregnancy losses, and Mrs. Lee was no exception. Having said that, there are certain steps we usually take as precautionary measures, including hormonal replacement treatment to support the pregnancy in case there is such a deficiency. We also consider the pregnancy to be a high-risk pregnancy due to what is generally labeled as "poor obstetrical history." I have always found such terminology, which only indicates our lack of understanding, inappropriate; at best, it is only useful as a reminder of our concern for the current pregnancy.

When Mrs. and Mr. Lee returned for their appointment, I shared the information about the laboratory results. I also tried to cautiously reassure them that, while the risk of a repeat loss has to be kept in mind, I could find nothing that concerned me. I explained the rationale for starting hormonal replacement and I laid out a care plan that involved mostly observation and continuous evaluation. I suggested that, until further notice, they should refrain from intercourse. Intercourse is a stimulant for the release of oxytocin, also known as labor hormone. Oxytocin can stimulate the uterus to contract—a situation that, under the circumstances, we wanted to avoid.

Mr. Lee smiled and told me that it in his culture it was traditional to avoid intercourse during pregnancy in order to avoid miscarriage, so that should not be a problem. He then asked if there were any dietary restrictions or special instructions. I said that there were none. I thought, however, that perhaps something customary made him ask the question, so inquired as to why he was concerned. Mr. Lee proceeded to tell me that pregnancy is considered a "hot" condition. in their tradition. Therefore, in order to keep the balance between Yin and Yang, the pregnant woman should eat "cold food." Caring for Mrs. Lee was turning out to be an educational experience for me, and an opportunity to learn something about Taiwanese cultural beliefs related to pregnancy. Such knowledge, I was sure, will allow me to care for Mrs. Lee and to have a better understanding of her culture.

I saw Mrs. Lee at regular intervals throughout her pregnancy. Repeated ultrasonographic studies showed the infant's growth curve as normal at all times. As a precautionary measure, after thirty-two weeks of pregnancy, we instituted twice weekly monitoring of the infant and I instructed Mrs. Lee to count fetal movements on a regular basis. I was extremely pleased that we were approaching term in what had been a perfectly normal pregnancy.

At one of the weekly visits during the last month of pregnancy, Mr. Lee asked if he could talk to me about the impending delivery. He wanted me to know that when labor began, he would be in the hospital but not in the delivery room. He explained that it was not the role of the father to participate in the delivery, and even if he had wanted to, his wife would not allow it. He also told me that it was his role, as the father, to give the baby its first bath. I told him I understood and that I would see if we could arrange for him to give the baby its first bath. Of course, that would be after the baby was cleaned immediately following birth in the delivery room. He understood that.

Mrs. Lee went into labor smiling and excited. Although I could have told her the sex of the baby, which was apparent on the ultrasound, she did not want to know. She was carrying a boy, which I knew would please both Mrs. and Mr. Lee, since the boy would carry on the family name.

During labor, Mrs. Lee's mother was present. Traditionally, her mother-in-law would accompany her daughter-in-law during labor, but as her elderly mother-in-law remained in Taiwan, Mrs. Lee's mother took her place. Mrs. Lee's mother was a lovely, softly spoken woman who had lived in the United States for most of her life. She asked me several times if everything was OK, and I was happy to reassure her that everything was proceeding as planned. I asked her if she would like to be present at delivery, and she said that she would.

During labor, Mrs. Lee was mostly silent. I knew from my recent cultural readings why. Not only would it be considered a sign of

167

weakness to be vocal, but crying during labor might also attract evil spirits to the infant; therefore, silence protects the baby.

As Mrs. Lee's contractions intensified and labor was progressing at a faster speed, I asked her if she would like an epidural to control her pain and discomfort. For a moment, Mrs. Lee and her mother silently exchanged eye contact, after which Mrs. Lee said: "No, thank you. I am well." Even at this point in her labor, Mrs. Lee did not utter a sound, and I believe that was the most she had said during her entire labor. I had also learned that in her culture it is not polite to accept something the first time it is offered. Therefore, some fifteen minutes later, I asked her again if she was sure she did not want an epidural. She assured me that she was all right. Two hours later, she delivered a six pound, eight ounces baby boy, who cried instantly. Both Mrs. Lee and her mother started crying simultaneously and I went to the waiting area to inform Mr. Lee that he was the father of a healthy boy. He smiled, shook my hand and said, "Thank you, thank you, thank you!" He then entered his wife's room.

Blanca

Blanca was a twenty-eight-year-old woman who was originally from the southern part of Brazil, near Porto Alegre, the capital city of the Brazilian state of Rio Grande do Sul. She was married, but her husband was home in Brazil and this was her first child. When she came to the hospital, she was already in early labor.

Blanca's English was not very good, but she managed to make herself understood and she was extremely happy when she learned that I could speak some Portuguese, so we could communicate in her native language. Her pregnancy had apparently been uncomplicated, her health had been good, and as far as she could tell, she was in her eight month of pregnancy. We figured that she was about thirty-four to thirty-five weeks gestation. After performing an ultrasound, we estimated the weight of the infant at about five to six pounds. I explained to her that we would try to stop labor, but that if we could not, the infant would most likely be fine.

We were able to control her contractions for a while, but evidently, her uterus was quite irritable. I suggested we perform an amniocentesis to determine whether the infant's lungs were mature, in which case, attempting to stop labor was pointless. She declined. The idea of placing a needle into her abdomen and removing some fluid from around the infant was entirely unacceptable to her. As an alternative, I suggested we give her a corticosteroid shot, as a precautionary measure, which would accelerate the infant's lung maturity, in case the lungs were not fully mature. She agreed to that.

We were able to control her contractions for a few days; over which time I had the opportunity to learn more about her. She was upset about her husband not being with her. He was a civil engineer back in Brazil and would not be able to leave from one day to another. She had been a few days away from returning home when her contractions had started. She wanted to know if I could give her some medication so that she could fly back home. I was pretty sure she would be in labor within the next twenty-four to thirty-six hours and a mid-air delivery at 30,000 feet was not an attractive proposition. I advised her against that alternative.

She then wanted to know who her doula was going to be. A doula is someone, usually a woman, who is trained to provide physical and emotional support during labor and delivery. Doulas do not provide any medical intervention, but they may act as advocates for the laboring woman's wishes, and communicate her desires to the medical staff. During labor, a doula may massage the laboring woman, help her change position, and in general act as a birth companion. She sometimes also provides support to the father and the family. In Brazil, two types of doulas are common. One is hospital-based, and the other is a private doula whom the family contracts to provide services to the future mother during labor and during the postpartum period. Sometimes, the doula will live within the household for a time after delivery.

Blanca was not happy when I told her that the hospital did not have doulas, and was distraught that she could not hire a doula privately either. When I asked her if her sister would be with her during delivery, she said that she would, but that her sister was not a doula.

I asked her if there was anything in particular that I could do for her. "Yes," she told me. "I do not want to have a cesarean section."
In Brazil, cesarean sections are almost the routine form of delivery and that country has one of the highest cesarean section rates in the world, close to 93% in private hospitals—the result of convenience, fad and economic incentives. I told Blanca I fully anticipated she would deliver vaginally, short of an unpredictable emergency. She was surprised, but relieved.
"When will I see the baby?" she asked.
"Immediately after birth," I said.
"Is that safe?"
"Perfectly safe," I told her. I knew from the ultrasound, that she was going to have a boy baby too, but she had not wanted to know the sex of the baby. "In case it is a boy," I asked, "do you want him circumcised?"
"Oh my God," she said. "Why do you want to do that?"
I explained to her that, in this country, circumcising baby boys was quite common. "No, no, no," she said emphatically.

As expected, Blanca went into labor the next day. Her waters broke and labor ensued without delay. Her sister was with her. She was a nice young woman, but I could see that she would not have been a good doula. Once labor started, Blanca was surprised at the minimal intervention. She had expected to receive an enema, which she did not. She had expected her perineum to be shaved, which we did not do. She had expected to be confined to bed for the entire duration of labor, rather than be allowed to move around until her labor was well advanced. She expected not be able to drink anything, but she was allowed to have ice chips. It seems that in Brazil, there is a protocol for all deliveries, and it is strictly followed. Furthermore, had she been in her home country, she probably would have ended up having a cesarean section, for reasons other than medical necessity.

As labor progressed, Blanca became quite vocal. I could follow the initiation of the contraction, its peak, and its subsequent disappearance by the tone and intensity of her cries. She was also rhythmically patting her abdomen during contractions, and the rhythm seemed to vary with each contraction. When the time came, I asked her if she would like an epidural. She knew what an epidural was all about, but was afraid of a needle in her back so she refused the epidural. Our nursing staff was wonderful and went above and beyond what they would normally do to ensure her labor went as smoothly as one could hope. She delivered a six pound, healthy boy.

Shortly after delivery, as she was holding her baby, Blanca asked to be left alone with him for a while. That was an unusual request, but seeing no problem with it, we all left the room. Her sister told us that she had wanted to explain to the baby why his father was not there, and to reassure him that, as soon as possible, they were going home.

Consuelo

Consuelo was from Lima, Peru, where her husband worked for the Peruvian Branch of an American company. They had been living in the United States for about a year while her husband was being trained for an executive position at the company's subsidiary in Peru. Both Consuelo and her husband were in their thirties, and this was their second child. Consuelo had suffered high blood pressure during her first pregnancy and remained mildly hypertensive after delivery. Because of that, she was referred to our office at twenty weeks gestation.

She had not suffered hypertension before she became pregnant with her first child, about two years ago. In this pregnancy, her high blood pressure appeared to be controlled with minimal medication. We talked about the significance of high blood pressure in pregnancy, the risk of it worsening or of her developing preeclampsia, and the concern that it may affect the infant's growth. I told her, however, that I believed her pregnancy will proceed smoothly in view of the minimal level of her high blood pressure.

171

Having lived in South America myself for about twenty years, many of Peru's problems with the delivery of obstetrical care were known to me. As most women lived away from the capital, in mountainous area where transport was difficult and few roads existed, home deliveries were the rule. Maternal mortality is high in Peru, about twenty to thirty times higher than in the United States. But I was not familiar with birthing customs or traditions, nor did I know to what extent these are still part of a routine delivery in Lima, Peru's largest city and Capital.

I asked Consuelo and her husband whether she planned to deliver here or whether she would return to Lima for the delivery. She told me that she would deliver here but that her mother would arrive to help her towards the end of pregnancy and after delivery.
"Is there anything in particular about your expected delivery that you would like me to know?" I asked.
"Yes," Consuelo responded. She told me that both her mother and her husband would be there during labor and delivery. I knew that in Peru, delivery traditionally occurs with the woman standing, supported by her husband. Consuelo knew this was not likely to happen here, but she wanted to be able to move during labor. I had no problem with that, assuming the labor progressed normally and that we could periodically monitor the infant. She agreed.

She also told me that her mother would want her to wear a special traditional belt around the abdomen, which was supposed to help control her pain. I had no problem with that and asked her if she would want an epidural, to which she replied she would decide when the time came. She also said it was customary for a laboring woman to drink a special local tea, which her mother would bring. Apparently, such beverage would prevent her having chills and would protect the infant. She also wanted to make sure that before I cut the umbilical cord, a tie would be placed toward her and another one toward the infant, although she could not tell me the significance of this tradition.

It did not seem to me that any of her desires would conspire against her care, so I told her I had no problem with any of her wishes, assuming labor progressed normally. Traditionally in Peru, the placenta is buried close to where the baby was delivered, but since she did not mention the placenta, I did not either. I considered that practicality had probably forced this custom to be abandoned in Lima.

Consuelo progressed through pregnancy with ease. Her blood pressure remained stable and we did not have to modify her medication. At around thirty-six weeks, her mother arrived from Peru and accompanied Consuelo on one of her visits. I guessed she was somewhere between fifty and sixty years old, but her Inca features made defining her age difficult. She was an extremely nice woman, who asked a lot of questions about her daughter's pregnancy. I assured her that everything was going well and that we did not expect any issues. When I inquired whether she would accompany her daughter during labor and delivery, she responded affirmatively, and added, "I will not be in your way with what I have to do."
Consuelo had already alerted me as to how her mother would be involved in her labor, so I nodded my head in agreement.

The last three weeks of Consuelo's pregnancy, although medically uneventful, were plagued by constant ill-defined complaints. From a nonspecific "I don't feel well" to "My mother thinks the baby has dropped," meaning, in medical terms, that the head has descended into the pelvis, a normal occurrence just before labor starts. There was an apparent progressive anxiety around when labor was going to start, which was difficult for me to grasp. I was unable to figure about this aspect of Consuelo's behavior and wondered whether it have had to do with her mother being there or due to a concern that something bad may happen towards the end of the pregnancy.

At around thirty-nine weeks, Consuelo went into labor. She arrived at the hospital at around 4 am on a Sunday morning. I arrived an hour later. My nurse greeted me with a smile and said with a wink, "Good Luck!"
I walked into Consuelo's room to discover that her mother had almost taken over the labor room. Colorful garlands surrounded

the bed and the table, on which a thermos was standing. I assumed it contained the ritual tea. Consuelo was walking around the room and intermittently sitting in the chair whenever a strong contraction did not allow her to walk. Her husband was walking with her. When a contraction occurred, he positioned himself behind her in an attempt to support her weight, something I knew was common for Peruvian women.

It was unusual, but I understood what was going on. I asked Consuelo to lie down so that I could examine her, and I called the nurse back into the room. Consuelo was in good labor and her waters had not yet broken. My examination confirmed that labor was progressing at a normal pace. I asked the nurse to monitor Consuelo for about fifteen minutes. Her mother immediately asked, "What's wrong?"
"Nothing," I said and reminded her that she promised not to interfere with what I had to do. I could tell that she was not pleased, but it was important for me that we reestablished each other's role.

The infant seemed fine, and I told the nurse we would monitor fifteen minutes of every hour, and in the interim, we would listen to the baby at regular intervals. I told Consuelo I would remain in the hospital for the duration of her labor, seeing her at regular intervals while the nurse would remain with her as needed.

I saw Consuelo about every hour. Things were progressing smoothly and as labor intensified Consuelo's mother placed a colorful belt, not unlike our monitoring belts only prettier, around her daughter's abdomen. Consuelo declined any pain medication. "The belt will do," she told me.
I never cease to be amazed by the power of suggestion. For Consuelo, at least for the time being, the belt was working, and that was the only thing that mattered! She never asked for any other pain medication and declined an epidural.

Consuelo continued to walk, followed by her husband, throughout the first part of her labor. At ten in the morning, the nurse called to tell me that she had broken her water. I asked the nurse to put a monitor on Consuelo and I rushed to the labor and delivery area.

Consuelo was sitting in bed, her husband on the edge of the bed behind her with his arms around her, and her mother, using a wet towel to wipe Consuelo's forehead. Once the contraction eased, I asked her to lie down so I could examine her. Her cervix was completely dilated and the baby's head had reached the perineum, which meant that delivery was imminent.

I shared my findings with Consuelo, her husband and her mother. Our labor rooms are almost instantly changed into a delivery room containing all one needs for a safe delivery. Consuelo objected to lying down, telling me she would feel when the baby was coming and at that time, and not before, she would lie down to allow me to deliver the baby. Short of restraining her, I had no choice but to agree, but I really did not think it would be a problem. With each contraction, as if following a script, her husband would sit behind her with his arm around her, as if they were for a standing delivery, and her mother would wipe her forehead. It was not long before she said, "It's coming," and instantly lay down. The head appeared, properly rotated, and was expelled with the next push. The rest of the body followed.
"It's a boy," I said.

What followed was unexpected. The three of them started laughing, crying and babbling to each other at the same time. The mother did a swing around the room, somewhere between a dance and a run. Her husband put his arms around Consuelo and kissed her.
"Don't forget to tie two strings on the cord," she reminded me. I certainly did so. I cut the cord and the placenta followed shortly afterward.

As the nurse was cleaning Consuelo and I was making sure that her birth canal was intact, her mother handed me a little plastic bag. "Will you please cut a piece of the placenta and put it in this bag for me?"
"Certainly," I said, as I thought to myself that, after all, traditions do not die, they just adapt.

* * *

Timing is everything

Webster dictionary defines timing as "the ability to select the precise moment for doing something for optimum effect." Occasionally, timing may be a little off, even if the effect is optimal.

Our obstetrical service had been seeing Veronica, a thirty-two-year-old woman now in her fifth pregnancy, throughout her pregnancy, although she had never quite understood our insistence on prenatal care. She was professionally driving a truck, making deliveries for a local distributor, so naturally, she missed many appointments, most of which had to be rescheduled more than once. Our nurse seemed to have to call her repeatedly. Veronica was one of these healthy, vigorous women, for whom pregnancy just happens. Labor and delivery were an inconvenience that she just had to put up with. All of her children had been fathered by the same boyfriend: Mike, a funny, hardworking electrician who drove a red Ford truck. Marriage was out of the question for Veronica. "It's not for me, that's all there is to it," she was known to have said many times.
As for her boyfriend, that was fine with him. "Whatever Veronica wants, Veronica gets," he once told me. They were quite a pair, but were obviously fond of each other and were always talking lovingly about their kids.

Veronica and her boyfriend lived out of town, maybe twenty to twenty-five miles from our hospital. She had a perfectly normal pregnancy, just like the other four.
"Here I am—for nothing," she used to tell us when she appeared for her prenatal visits. Our staff established quite a bond with Veronica, whom they referred to as "that character."

Although her obstetrical history was such that another normal pregnancy was to be expected, as always, we were concerned about potential problems that might occur when least expected. Having numerous pregnancies is known to predispose women to certain complications, particularly very fast labor, postpartum hemorrhage,

and a few others. What's more, during the last pregnancy, Veronica had arrived at the hospital just thirty minutes before delivery. We do not particularly like that, so we were sometimes wondering whether Veronica might be an accident waiting to happen.
"You are too concerned about the whole thing. I'll be OK. What's the big deal? I will have another child," she had said many times, dismissing us in the process.

To her credit, for the last six weeks, Veronica had been faithfully attending all her appointments. Sometimes, her boyfriend would even come with her. "Everything OK, doc?" her boyfriend used to ask. "Stop bugging the doctor. Of course I'm fine," she would admonish him.
She was right; she was fine, and we were pleased.

At one of her visits, she discussed their decision that five kids were enough. After this delivery, she wanted to have her tubes tied. "Could you do it?" she asked.
I asked her what she knew about tying tubes.
Veronica looked at me as if not quite believing my question. "Of course, I won't get pregnant anymore. Isn't that so?"
"Yes," I replied, "but you need to know some more about it."
I wanted to make sure she understood that tubal ligation is a permanent procedure. Should she ever change her mind and want another child, reversing the procedure, although possible, has a very low chance of success. Tying the tubes can also create surgical complications, even if the chances of that were very, very low.

Veronica understood and had no questions.
"When can I have it?" she asked.
"The day after delivery," I told her.
She was pleased and had no other questions.
As we approached her due date, Veronica called several times to tell us she had experienced contractions and that she thought labor was starting. We asked her to come in to be checked out. She came the first time, but was not in labor, and she returned home a little disappointed. A couple of days later, she called again. Again, we suggested she should come in.

"No," was the answer. "I'll see what happens for a while. If it gets worse, I'll be there."
We did not see her that day, so we assumed that she quieted down again.

Two days later, she came for a regular prenatal visit. We were only three days away from her due date and her examination showed, unequivocally, that the previous contractions had changed her cervix. It was now very thin and partially opened. The head of the baby was also applied against it, which meant only one thing: labor was about to start any minute! Furthermore, with a history of prior fast labor, I thought it was prudent for her to remain at the hospital. If she did not go into labor by the next morning, I could start her labor, but I thought it would start without any problems. Hers was not a situation where going home made any sense, and it could only create problems should labor start suddenly and vigorously, as she would not make to the hospital if that were to happen.

After reflecting for a moment, Veronica said she did not want to stay in the hospital and nor did she want to have her labor started. She preferred to wait.
"I'll make it here, don't worry," she assured me. "Mike is a super driver. He'll get me here. I am going home, that's that." She stood up, ready to get dressed.
"Hold on, Veronica," I told her. "This is not that simple. I cannot, in all conscience, discharge you. I have seen this before and it is not safe for you or the baby," I admonished her. "I bet you that if I strip your membranes, you would go into labor in no time."
"Nope. Doc, if you won't let me go, I'll sign myself out. I don't want any membranes stripped. It's my problem."
I insisted. "Veronica, do not do that. I'll deliver you by tomorrow, I promise. I'm concerned for you and your baby," I said.
"Nope. I'm going."

Veronica signed herself out. I was not happy. It was an occasion when being hardheaded, which worked for Veronica at most times in her life, was a wrong decision. I hoped she might prove me wrong, but the best I could hope was that the following day, if not overnight, she would go into labor and get to the hospital on time.

Early the next morning, I was making rounds when I received a call from the head nurse in the labor and delivery area. Mike, Veronica's boyfriend, was frantic on the phone. Veronica was in very good labor, and he was rushing in his pickup truck with Veronica next to him. We figured that they were about ten miles from the hospital. I had the call transferred so I could talk to Mike. "How close are her contractions?" I asked.
"Every three minutes or less. Can you send an ambulance to meet us?"
"Stay on the line and let me ask." I got his exact location and called the ambulance service, which always has at least one ambulance by the hospital emergency room. They did not think they could do it. Mike was on a four-lane highway with intermittent exits every six or seven miles. There was no way could they coordinate that. The dispatcher had, however, a good idea that was worth trying. It was to call the state police. If they had someone in the vicinity, a trooper could ride ahead of them, sirens blaring, so they can drive as fast as they could.

I told Mike what had transpired and asked him to stay on the line. Moments later, the dispatcher told me that a trooper was in the area and on his way to catch them. Once Mike sees the trooper's flashing lights, coming from behind him, he should put his hazard lights on and follow the trooper.
"God bless you," said Mike and hang up.

Our job was just beginning. I asked the head nurse to send one of the labor and delivery nurses downstairs to the parking lot next to the emergency room and for her to bring an emergency delivery pack. Emergency delivery packs contain sterile drapes, gloves, an infant resuscitation kit, and some basic surgical instruments and are used when delivery occurs without the time to open a delivery room. I indicated I would meet the nurse downstairs in the emergency room.

We estimated that, if everything went well, they should arrive at the hospital shortly. While we were waiting, the nurse asked who the patient was.

"Her name is Veronica," I told her.

"Oh yes, I remember. She is the lady who signed herself out yesterday."

I told her that, indeed, it was the same patient.

"Oh my!"

We waited for about ten minutes before we heard the sirens of the state police. As it turned out, there were two of them—one in front and one behind Mike's red truck. I later learned that the first trooper had called another trooper, just to make sure they could bring Mike safely in.

Mike parked his truck in the middle of the parking lot, jumped out and yelled at us, "Over here! Over here!"

Figuring that Veronica wouldn't make it to the emergency room door, the nurse and I ran toward the truck, and an orderly followed us, pushing a gurney. In the meantime, the two troopers placed their cars in the front and back of Mike's truck, with their flashing lights and sirens at full blast, to keep curious onlookers away. They also directed the traffic in the parking lot away from us.

As soon as we reached the truck, Mike was back in it attempting to comfort Veronica. Upon opening the truck's door, we found her lying on her back with her head in Mike's lap. "It's coming. It's coming," she said. She was wearing a night-gown, fortunately. The nurse pulled the gurney closer to the truck, placed her emergency pack on it, and opened it without delay, She gave me my gloves, which I barely had time to put on before Veronica took a deep breath and pushed the baby out into my waiting hands. I took the baby, rapidly cut the cord, and handed the infant, a boy, to the nurse, who wrapped him and aspirated his nostrils and mouth to remove any remaining mucus and fluid. The baby cried instantly.

By that time, a crowd of some fifty people had gathered around us, beyond the cordon placed by the troopers. Everyone started applauding and screaming out, "Yay."

We placed Veronica on the gurney.

"Are you examining her in the emergency room?" the nurse asked me.

"Yes. Please have everything ready. I will be there in a minute," I answered as she and the orderly pushed the gurney toward ER. In the rush, the metal box of the pack had been left behind. I took it, wrapped it in the remaining available towels, and went to thank the troopers.

They were relatively young men, probably in their late twenties, early thirties at most. "Good job, gentlemen," I said. "I appreciate it, and most certainly the patient appreciates it."

They both answered almost simultaneously, "Not a problem. Glad to be of help."

"Quite a night, I must say," said one. "Wait till I tell my wife that I was a stork tonight."

We all started laughing.

I still had to take care of the placenta, and most importantly, check Veronica for any tears or problem associated with her fast labor and ordeal. When I entered the ER surgical room, a couple of nurses from labor and delivery were cleaning and washing Veronica. She was calm, composed, and apparently had no complaints. The baby was in the nearby crib. Veronica just looked at me and said, "I don't want to hear it. You were right."

"OK," I answered without further comment. I proceeded to tell her that I would have to perform an internal examination to make sure the rapid labor had not produced any damage to her birth canal. An anesthesiologist entered and asked if he was needed.

"Some sedation for discomfort, would help, thank you," I told him. A few minutes later, after starting intravenous fluids, he administered a sedative to Veronica. I removed the placenta, which had already detached and was in the vagina. Her birth canal was intact and so was the uterus and cervix.

I wrote some orders and asked the nurses to move Veronica upstairs to the labor and delivery area. Veronica was sleeping peacefully.

Mike was as pale as a white wall. "Is she OK?" he asked, once he saw me entering the emergency waiting room.

"Yes, Mike. Everything is fine. The baby boy is fine and Veronica is being taken upstairs to the labor and delivery area. Follow me and you can see her."

We walked upstairs to the third floor. On the way up, I heard Mike ask, "Once again, she had it her way, doc. What do you do with a woman like that?"

"Love her," I told him.

He smiled and shook his head.

Veronica had a good day and slept well all night. In the morning, when I went to see her, she asked me when I would perform the tubal ligation.

"It's not going to happen today," I told her. "Your delivery occurred in the truck in the parking lot. You'll be OK, but the environment of your delivery was far from being sterile. I cannot risk the remote possibility of you having an infection. Performing surgery under the circumstances would be a big mistake. No arguments, please," I said.

This time, she did not argue. She remained silent for a while, and then simply said, "Thank you for everything."

Veronica recovered quickly after her delivery. The infant, an eight-pound boy, was doing well and the neonatologist did not think he had to stay in hospital but could go home with his mother. I kept Veronica in for another day, and she went home happy and looking forward to her tubal ligation in about six weeks.

It had been a day to remember.

Unforgettable moments

In the course of human interaction—the essence of the relationship between patient and physicians, especially between an expectant mother and her obstetrician—there are moments that, by their very nature, are as brief as they are unforgettable. The moment a woman becomes a mother, something very special happens in her mind and in the way she looks at life. She is, simultaneously, overwhelmed by the birth of her baby and by indescribable feelings, not only for her baby but for the world around her. At that point in time, it is not unusual that a word, an action, or a statement, can leave an indelible impression. Throughout my career, I have had the privilege of experiencing many such special moments, a few of which I would like to share.

I remember, as if it were yesterday, the day that Peggy, who had lost her vision in a terrible childhood accident, delivered a little girl. Peggy had been the most stoic patient I'd ever had and had delivered after a long, difficult labor, which was exhausting to her as well as to those around her. Her husband had been at her side throughout. He was encouraging, supportive and loving.

Seconds after the baby was born, the infant's cries filled the room. I showed the baby to the father, who took her in his arms and approached his exhausted wife. "She is beautiful. She is beautiful," he kept saying. Then he took the little girl and gently placed her in his wife's arms. "Look at her, she is beautiful!" he said again.

Peggy held the baby in her arms. Then, gently, as if holding a fine piece of porcelain, she started touching the baby with her right hand. First at the top her head, down her face, eyes, nose, mouth, then caressing the top of her head again and touching every finger of the infant's little hands and the toes of her tiny feet.

All who were present—nurses, her husband, and myself—froze in time. You could not hear us breathing. We knew that we were experiencing a magical moment. Her husband had tears in his eyes and I know that both of the nurses were fighting theirs, as was I.

183

It took Peggy what seemed like an eternity. She then smiled, kissed her baby and said, "Yes, she is beautiful." It was clear that Peggy did not need her eyes to see her daughter. Her gentle touch allowed her to have a mental image of her baby. Somehow, she was able to see what others with perfect vision may sometimes miss. I knew that was one baby girl who would have a wonderful mother.

* * *

Alison was a twenty-three years old and been married for no more than a year. Sometime after their wedding, her husband, Peter, had been drafted to the Vietnam War. At the time of his drafting, Alison was already pregnant. A few months after being sent to Vietnam, Pete was killed in action. There she was, a very young widow, pregnant and alone. Throughout her pregnancy, Alison mourned her young husband and talked at length about him. Her pregnancy progressed smoothly and she delivered a healthy baby boy of seven pounds, thirteen ounces. She decided to name him Peter, after his father. Throughout her labor, Alison kept her husband's picture, taken in his army uniform, by her bed.

The morning after her son's birth, I was making rounds on my patients when I reached Alison's room. After gently knocking on the door, I entered to find Alison sitting in an armchair, facing the window. The chair was next to a small table that held her late husband's picture. She was talking to the baby, which she cradled in her arms, and she had not heard me enter the room.
"Pete, little boy, this is your daddy. He was a hero, and will never come back. He is by the side of God, looking after us." There was a long pause, and then she was sobbing. "Pete, my love," she said, looking at the picture. "This is our son, Pete Jr. He is beautiful. He will grow up to be strong, and I promise you he will know and never forget who his father was." She burst into tears.

Slowly and silently, I backed out of the room. I could not interrupt that precious moment for Alison and her son. She needed to be alone for some time with her baby and her memories. Rounds could wait.

* * *

Tammy was paraplegic. She had been born with a severe congenital anomaly known as spina bifida. Spina bifida presents as an opening in the lower part of the person's back, which exposes the spinal cord. Today, surgery can be performed on an infant following its birth, thus diminishing the potential problems associated with this anomaly, but when Tammy had been born, doctors had not even known whether she would survive and she had grown up as a paraplegic. Later in life, Tammy had undergone some surgery to close the opening in her back, but the damage had already been done. Her surgery, at least, allowed her to live without the constant fear of infection.

Tammy was now pregnant and her husband had come with her for her prenatal visits. He was caring, and they obviously had a loving relationship.

At the first visit, we went into the examining room and I asked two nurses to help me move Tammy from the wheelchair to the examining table.
Her husband intervened. "I am used to moving her. Let me do it." He went to the wheelchair and lifted Tammy into his arms, gently moving her to the table and giving her a kiss. "There you are, sweetheart," he said. "Are you comfortable?"

"Yes, thank you," she said with a smile.
Over time, I have seen hundreds of couples interact with each other, but that short exchange between Tammy and her husband spoke volumes, and told me this was a very special relationship.

* * *

Prudence had lost two prior pregnancies, both early in gestation.
The baby of her third pregnancy had died of SIDS, or Sudden
Infant Death Syndrome. Her fourth pregnancy now was coming
close to term. We did not anticipate any problems, but Prudence
was concerned about labor. What if something happened?
"Could I have a cesarean section, just to be sure?"
We reassured her that she would be OK. "We will do a cesarean
section if it becomes necessary," I told her.

She went into labor and delivered a healthy little girl. As soon
as I tied and cut the cord, I placed the little girl in her arms. Her
husband had been with her throughout labor. They were both in
awe. They kissed each other and he placed his head on her shoulder
and started crying. She caressed his face and started crying as
well. "We'll call her Hope," Prudence said.

The little girl will probably never know why her parents named her
Hope. But at that point in time, hope is what they had, and needed.
The little girl embodied their hope that this child would live a long
and happy life. What a wonderful choice of name.

* * *

When Polly first came to see me, we both knew she should not
have become pregnant. Polly had a major heart problem and her
cardiologist had advised her against pregnancy. Her heart condition
was so bad that she had been placed on a cardiac transplant
patient list. In spite of that, she became pregnant and I first saw
her when her pregnancy was already at twenty-two weeks. During
her pregnancy, Polly was in and out of the hospital many times.
Her husband was a nervous wreck. He had called me repeatedly,

and once bluntly asked if I thought she would make it through pregnancy. What if a heart became available while she was pregnant? What would we do?

But Polly had faith, unshakable faith.

When she went into labor, we delivered her in the cardiac intensive care unit, with her husband by her side. She delivered uneventfully, a boy, six pounds, nine ounces. As soon as she delivered, I placed the baby in her arms. She took him, caressed him, gave him a kiss, and then turned to her husband and said, "Wasn't all this worthwhile? Now we can wait for the heart transplant. God is with me."

I never cease to be amazed at how faith can carry people through their most trying times. Polly carried her pregnancy and delivered a healthy baby, against all odds. She had the best medical care, but deep down I think Polly would have made it no matter what: her deep faith sustained her.

* * *

Drew had been a diabetic since age three. Growing up had not been easy for her. Her diabetes had taken some toll on her general health, but now, at twenty-four years of age, she was pregnant and was doing OK. Her pregnancy had some ups and downs, which we were able to handle, and carried her close to term. She was not married and her boyfriend was not involved.
"I don't care," she once told me. "It's his loss. He disappeared the moment I told him I was pregnant."

Drew's father had died a few years before, but her mother, a very pleasant woman, had been supportive of her. By thirty-eight weeks, we decided it was time to deliver the baby. An induction was started. Labor progressed without incident, and by afternoon, she delivered a baby girl, eight pounds, nine ounces.

As we were finishing the delivery, the clerk arrived and told Drew that someone by the name of Alec had arrived and wanted permission to come into the room. He claimed to be the father of the baby. How he found out she was in labor, we never knew.

Drew, without a moment of hesitation, told the clerk. "I don't want to see him. Tell him he is not a father; he was just a sperm donor. He is not welcome here. Tell him to leave."

Drew obviously had deep feelings about what a father was and should be, not only to the baby, but to his partner, the mother. She was right. There was little doubt that his lack of involvement during pregnancy was a bad omen for their future, and Drew did not want any part of it.

* * *

Alberta was twenty-six and in her second pregnancy. Her husband, a career army officer, had been deployed overseas, and she had been unable to accompany him for some reason. Her first pregnancy had ended in an emergency cesarean section as a result of the infant not having tolerated labor, which was due to the baby's cord being around its neck.

This pregnancy was proceeding normally, and she hoped to be able to deliver vaginally. Assuming everything would be fine, I saw no reason to object to her wishes. On one occasion, her husband was on leave and was able to attend the office with her. He was a very nice gentleman, who hoped he might be able to be present for the delivery. He only needed twenty-four hours notice, and he would be able to catch a military plane to be by her side.

That, of course, was easier said than done. A cesarean section can be scheduled, but a spontaneous delivery—not really. Should she need an emergency cesarean delivery, we would not be able to wait, although I did not anticipate that.

"Then I will just have to be here the next day," he told me. Alberta understood, but she hoped that even with her having a vaginal delivery, perhaps he would be present.

When Alberta went into labor, she called her husband to let him know even before she arrived at hospital. He told her that the next plane he could catch was in the morning, so he would be with her late in the afternoon.

Alberta arrived at the hospital very early in the morning and I arrived shortly after her, at around six am. She was in very early labor, and in fact, given her mild contractions, I would not have been surprised if it were a false alarm.

Alberta told me her husband would be arriving sometime in the afternoon and she wanted to know what were the chances of her delivering before he arrived.
"Frankly," I told her. "At the present time, I'm not even sure you are in labor. Once labor is more established, I will be in a better position to predict a possible time of delivery." Traditionally, obstetricians rarely, if ever, like to predict time of delivery.

Her contractions continued to be mild but steady. By ten o'clock that morning she had started to make progress and was in labor.
"Still no predictions?" she asked.
I told her that she was in very good labor and that, if nothing changed, by afternoon she should be delivering.
"I have to slow down," she told me. "Charlie will not be here before late afternoon. Could you slow down the labor?"
"This kind of labor, we can't stop," I told her.
Alberta was not happy.
"I'll have to slow down," she kept repeating to herself. "I have to slow down."

Considering the complexity of the brain and its control on the many functions related to labor, I did not discard the possibility she might be able to slow her labor, even if I did not know how she would go about that.

At two o'clock, Alberta received a telephone call from her husband. He was half an hour away from landing, which meant he was about an hour or so from reaching the hospital.

"I'm holding," I heard her telling her husband. "Hurry!"

I had to leave labor and delivery to see a patient who had been admitted in emergency, so I told the nurse in charge of Alberta, Tina, where to reach me. Fortunately, the problem in the ER was neither serious nor an emergency, so on the way back to labor and delivery, I stopped in to the cafeteria for a snack, since I hadn't yet had lunch.

When I returned to labor and delivery, I asked Tina how Alberta was doing.

"Quiet," she answered.

"What does that mean?"

"It means that her contractions have slowed down," Tina said.

I guess she took special pleasure in my puzzled expression.

"Her contractions have all but vanished. Want to check her?" she added.

"Well, my curiosity is in high gear," I said

We both entered Alberta's room, arriving at the peak of a contraction. Alberta hardly acknowledged the discomfort. My examination showed her to have progressed little since my last examination, about two hours before.

"I think I'll make it," Alberta said. "My labor slowed down a little bit." She smiled.

Right then, her phone rang. "Wonderful," she said, and then addressed Tina and me. "Charlie is at the airport." Turning back to the phone, she said, "I'm great. Don't waste time; come directly here. The baby has been holding for you."

I was pleased for her. Whether it was a coincidence, or one of those occasional situations where labor slows for a while for no apparent reason, or whether Alberta's willpower had something to do with what happened, I do not know. The fact remains that Alberta will always think she managed to delay her labor so that her husband could be present at the birth of their child—and that is really the only thing that matters

Alberta had a baby boy, eight pounds, three ounces, shortly after her husband arrived at the hospital.

Even in the absence of scientific evidence, most of us have seen circumstances where the patient's willpower may have altered the expected course of clinical evidence. Alberta was determined to have her husband at her side at the time of delivery. I am glad she achieved her goal.

* * *

SECTION 4:

IN A CLASS OF THEIR OWN

A mother's secret

There are many factors in our blood that make each of us unique. Everyone has heard stories of people receiving transfusions of "the wrong blood type," which means that the transfused blood did not match the one of the patient. One blood factor that is important during pregnancy is the Rh factor. If both parents are Rh positive or Rh negative, there are no problems. However, if the father is positive and the mother negative, it can have disastrous consequences for the baby. Why?

During pregnancy, some of the baby's red blood cells pass into the mother's circulation. If the baby is Rh positive and the mother is Rh negative, her immune system goes on alert because the Rh positive cells of the baby are foreign to the mother. Her immune system will create antibodies against the Rh positive factor and, in order to protect the mother, will mount an attack against the baby's Rh positive factor. This will destroy the circulating foreign red cells.

Antibodies meant to destroy the few red cells from the baby that entered the mother's circulation, also cross to the baby. Since the baby is Rh positive, these antibodies also begin to destroy the baby's red cells. The result is that the baby will become anemic, and in extreme cases, will die. After birth, the maternal antibodies against the Rh factor continue to be present in her circulation. In subsequent pregnancies, the reaction becomes stronger; thus, with each pregnancy the destruction of the fetal red cells worsens.

The multiple inheritance possibilities created by Rh factor are quite complex. Suffice to say that if the father is Rh positive, and the mother is Rh negative, the infant will be Rh positive. This is because, genetically, the Rh positive factor is dominant. The infant will also, however, inherit the Rh negative factor from the mother.

Prior to 1940, when the Rh factor was discovered, when dead and anemic babies were born, the cause for those deaths was not understood. Usually, it was attributed to other causes, including syphilis. Once the Rh factor issue became known, it was only a matter of time before treatment and prevention became available. In babies who were anemic before birth, intrauterine transfusions, performed several times during pregnancy, were literally saving babies from dying in utero. Today, the disease is quite rare. Mothers who are Rh negative receive Rhogam, an injection of antibodies that destroys the circulating fetal red cells which have crossed into the maternal circulation. Rhogam prevents the maternal production of antibodies to combat the Rh factor, and thus protects the baby's red cells from being destroyed. Today, all Rh negative pregnant women who do not have antibodies against the Rh factor circulating in their blood, receive Rhogam.

Long before Rhogam became available, Grace became a patient of mine. Her family physician referred her to me after her first pregnancy, primarily because of an Rh problem. Subsequently, she had two other pregnancies. In each pregnancy, the severity of the baby's anemia increased, and in both pregnancies, I had to transfuse the baby several times over the course of gestation. Now, she was pregnant again.

For her first office visit, Grace and her husband arrived together and wanted to know what their chances were of having another healthy baby. I fully expected that I would have to transfuse their infant several times before delivery, which increased the chances of complications. Grace's husband, however, was optimistic. He had read somewhere that the woman's body gets used to the problem with subsequent pregnancies, and therefore thought that this new baby would be all right. My attempts to explain why this was unlikely, failed to change his mind.
"Doctors do not always know everything," he told me.
I could not argue with the general statement; however, we knew very well how the Rh disease worked and I explained that to him again.
"We'll see," he said.

At her next visit, Grace was alone. I wanted to make sure she understood what we were facing. She understood, but she hoped for the best. Grace's pregnancy was about twelve weeks along at that time. I shared my management plans and emphasized that we would probably need to start intrauterine transfusions earlier than we had with her earlier pregnancies. She nodded, but did not say anything.

In the early seventies, we did not have the benefit of ultrasound. Our only way of assessing the infants of Rh negative mothers was by performing sequential amniocentesis and quantifying the level of bilirubin in the amniotic fluid. Bilirubin is the product of the destroyed fetal red cells. The more bilirubin we found, the more severe the infant's anemia. This correlation worked quite well and allowed us to perform the intrauterine transfusion before the anemia became critical or life-threatening.

By the twenty-fourth week of Grace's pregnancy, I performed the first amniocentesis. To my surprise, the study of the fluid was reported as normal. I requested the laboratory repeat the study to ensure it was not an error. It was not.

Normal amniotic fluid was unusual under these clinical circumstances. During her previous pregnancies, we had tested her husband to determine whether, although he was Rh positive, he happened to carry an Rh negative gene, too. If that had been the case, Grace would have had a 50% chance of having an Rh negative baby, which would have required no transfusions. He did not—Grace had no chance of having an Rh negative baby. I could not explain the findings of the first amniocentesis, so I shared my thoughts with Grace and we decided to repeat the amniocentesis in two week's time.

The second amniocentesis was also reported as normal. Grace told me after knowing the results that she would prefer not to have any further amniocentesis during the pregnancy, and that she was confident she would be all right. She was calm and composed without a sign of worry on her face. At one point, I even thought I saw a faint smile on her face.

A thought crossed my mind that perhaps she knew something I did not, and it occurred to me that this baby might not be her husband's child. She did not confide in me and I did not feel I could intrude into her private life, but one thing was sure, this baby was normal.

The rest of her pregnancy was perfectly uneventful. She asked me if she could have her tubes tied after this delivery. She did not want any more children. I thought that was a wise decision, and told her that I could most certainly do that if that was what she wanted. She indicated that it was.

Grace went into labor a day before her due date. After having had several children, her labor progressed quickly. She delivered a baby girl, who cried immediately. Sometime after the baby's birth, the pediatrician told me the baby was Rh negative—a genetic impossibility in view of the fact that her husband was Rh positive. My suspicion had been confirmed: her husband was not the father.

The next day, she had her tubes tied. In those days, women remained in hospital for four or five days after a delivery. Every day, I went to see her. She was happy but she never said a word. On the day of her discharge from the hospital, her husband was in the room. I greeted him, and he said, smiling, "Well, doc, I was right." "Yes," I replied, "you were right. Doctors do not always know everything."
He laughed.

I told Grace I would write the discharge orders, and come to see her again with some written instructions and a prescription for pain medication, just in case she felt uncomfortable from the tubal ligation surgery. When I returned to her room, her husband had gone to bring their car around to the main hospital entrance.

I gave Grace her prescriptions and postpartum instructions and told her I would like to see her again in six weeks. She nodded. As I said goodbye and turned to leave the room, she grabbed my arm. Fighting back tears, she said, "I have a confession to make. You probably know this baby is not my husband's baby, and you are right, but not in the way you may think. I don't want you to believe I was unfaithful. I love my husband dearly. I got pregnant with this baby by artificial insemination. My husband did not want me to tell anybody, but I need to tell you that now. Four years ago, we decided not to have any more children and he had a vasectomy. Then, tragedy struck, and my oldest child died in a car accident. As time went by, we wanted another child and we went to a fertility specialist. He suggested several alternatives, including artificial insemination. We opted to go that route. Because of my Rh history, they made sure the donor was Rh negative. I am ever so sorry not to have been straightforward with you from the beginning, but my husband is very sensitive to the fact that he is not the father of this baby and he absolutely did not want anyone to know. Please forgive us."

Her story was moving and I thanked her for confiding in me.

"I needed to tell you the truth for my own pride and self-respect. I hope you understand."

"I most certainly do," I replied. "I am very sorry about the loss of your child."

A labor of love

Once, a young couple came to my office after receiving bad news from their doctor. Their baby had a congenital anomaly of the central nervous system that was known as "anencephaly." This is a rare, fatal condition.

Shortly after conception, an embryo begins to develop what's known as a neural tube, which eventually gives rise to the nervous system. By the third or fourth week of pregnancy, the neural tube, which is initially open, closes. Sometimes, this closure does not happen, resulting in a variety of malformations known as open neural tube defects. The most serious is anencephaly, where the lack of closure is at the head, preventing a large portion of the brain and skull from developing. Anencephalic infants die before or during birth, or within hours or days of delivery. Anencephaly occurs in only about 1 in 10,000 births in the United States.

They had two other children, girls age nine and five, and both previous pregnancies had been normal. There was no family history of any congenital anomalies on either side. The woman was about fourteen weeks pregnant when she and her husband first met with me. Understandably, they were in shock.

As a precaution, I repeated an ultrasound exam to confirm the findings. They wanted to understand the ultrasound images, so I showed them images as we performed the ultrasound and explained exactly what we were looking at. She had tears in her eyes and gripped her husband's hand.

After completing the ultrasound, we went into my office to discuss the options. In circumstances like this, where the malformation is clearly fatal, doctors usually advise ending the pregnancy. Continuing the pregnancy carries certain risks that may put the mother in jeopardy, only to have either a stillborn or an infant who dies shortly after birth. For example, the excessive amount of amniotic fluid common to these kinds of pregnancies can lead to dangerous complications for the mother. Delivery can be traumatic too, because these infants usually have broad shoulders and can get stuck in the pelvis. Allowing such pregnancies to continue is generally not in the best interest of the mother.

They both listened attentively as I explained all this. Then they asked a few questions and said they would have to think about what path to take. They also wanted to discuss it with their families and with their pastor. A week later, they returned to my office and told me they had decided to continue the pregnancy. Both fully understood the risks associated with that decision.

The pregnancy continued uneventfully until about the thirty-second week. An ultrasound showed large pockets of fluid inside the uterus, and baby looked as if he were floating in slow motion in a sea of water. I was surprised when she asked, "Is the baby OK?" Her hand touched the screen at the site where the infant's image appeared, as if she wanted to feel the baby.
I was moved by her gesture and did not immediately answer her question. "I know my baby has a problem," she continued. "I am not in denial, but he is still my baby."
"The baby is OK," I answered. I kept the image up onscreen for her for a long time.

The next few weeks were difficult. The size of her uterus made moving uncomfortable and it partially blocked her blood circulation, causing her legs to swell. Her large abdomen interfered with breathing and made it hard for her to lie down and sleep. She began spending the night upright in an armchair.

Labor began at thirty-four weeks, when her water broke at home. Once in the hospital, they asked me if the baby was still alive. If so, they wanted him to be monitored so they could listen to his heartbeat throughout labor. We usually do not do this when we know the baby is unlikely to survive. My concern with her request was that if the baby's heart stopped and he died during labor, it might be too upsetting for them. Throughout the pregnancy, I had come to know both of them quite well, so I explained my concerns. Both said that it would be no different to having the baby die in their arms after birth. Their entire attitude throughout the

201

pregnancy was thoughtful and caring, and they both deeply loved their child. I couldn't deny their request.

Our nurses were moved by their story and went out of their way to make labor as comfortable as possible. Labor progressed quite rapidly and she delivered within hours. The baby boy was born alive. Nurses cleaned him, dressed him, put a little knitted bonnet on his open head, wrapped him in a blanket, and placed him in his mother's arms.

Soon, their two daughters and their pastor arrived. The pastor baptized the infant and for the next several hours, the couple and their daughters were left alone with the baby.

During that time, I talked for quite some time with their pastor, a middle-aged gentleman who seemed kind and very fond of both of them.
"I am sure it was not easy," I said.
"No," replied the pastor, "but they are a loving couple, deeply attached to their children, and they did not think this child should be any different."
A few hours later, the infant died in his mother's arms, with his father and his two sisters at his side.

* * *

Against the odds

When one talks about pregnancy complications, most people think about the possibility of a miscarriage, diabetes, high blood pressure, prematurity, and maybe a few others. The truth is, even if they have heard of such complications, future mothers never, ever, think it might be happening to them. This is the result of a self-defense mechanism. We always think other people have complications, not us; otherwise, who would want to get pregnant?

Of course, there are a great number of complications of pregnancy than most people know about. That is why Lillian was shocked when she learned what type of pregnancy she carried.

The fertilized egg travels to the uterus and implants itself into the uterine muscle and eventually fills the entire uterine cavity where it stays for nine months until delivery occurs, sometimes, it does not reach the uterus and remains in the fallopian tube, becoming an ectopic pregnancy. Because it is not in the uterus but in the tube, these are also known as "tubal pregnancies." An ectopic pregnancy is a dangerous condition, but it is usually rapidly resolved, either because it ruptures and the consequent bleeding becomes an emergency that requires surgery, or nowadays, it is diagnosed by ultrasound before it ruptures and medication can be started to make the pregnancy resorb. As rare as this may be, it is not the rarest of ectopic pregnancies. Much, much rarer is when the fertilized egg, after being fertilized in the tube, instead of progressing to the uterus, is expelled from the tube into the abdominal cavity. When that happens, it becomes what is known as an abdominal pregnancy. Abdominal pregnancies happen in just 1 in 10,000 pregnancies, and some suggest they are even rarer than that. Some obstetricians might not see a single case throughout their entire career.

Lillian was a mother of two. This was her third pregnancy and her two earlier pregnancies had raised no problems, so it was a shock to her when her obstetrician referred her to our office.

SILVIO ALADJEM MD

An abdominal pregnancy is a very serious and potentially life-threatening situation. Since the egg is not inside the uterus, the placenta is unable to implant in the muscle of the uterine wall so that it can start developing. Therefore, the placenta attaches itself wherever it can find blood vessels that will provide the necessary oxygen and nutrients for the baby. It becomes a matter of survival for the baby, and as a result the placenta starts attaching to the maternal pelvis, on a loop of the bowels, or elsewhere within the abdominal cavity. Instead of having a localized placenta that eventually occupies almost one fourth of the uterus, the placenta will extend to the mother's abdominal organs, seeking a way to provide nutrients and oxygen to the fetus.

Lillian was only fourteen weeks pregnant when she came to us. Her obstetrician had made the diagnosis of an abdominal pregnancy at a routine early ultrasound, so Lillian had no idea what was going to happen next. Unsure she knew or did not know, we explained to both Lillian and her husband what we were dealing with. It was difficult for them to conceive the idea of an abdominal pregnancy. They had a lot of questions: What had gone wrong? Why did that happen? Would the baby be all right? What were the risks to Lillian? Would she be able to have more children after this one? While all these questions were to be expected, and are questions that any rational individual would raise, not all can be answered directly with yes or no. What we attempted to do, instead, was to answer their questions and discuss the risks if Lillian were to continue the pregnancy. In pregnancy, few decisions are risk free. If the pregnancy was allowed to continue, the delivery would have to be by a cesarean section and the placenta would have to be left behind, which carries additional risks. Abdominal pregnancy is not a condition of mitigating consequences. It was important I give them a clear understanding of what to expect, since decisions would have to be made, risks pondered, and consequences realistically understood.

Their visit with me lasted an hour or more. At the end, Lillian said she now understood how serious her condition was, but she needed some time to think and to make a decision. Her husband was a

204

little bit more decisive.

"What is there to think about?" he said. "I do not want to become a widower and the children do not want to be orphans."

"I know," she answered. "That is why I have to think about all of this."

Pregnancy is a remarkable event for a mother-to-be. I knew exactly what Lillian was thinking. She had to choose between losing the child she was carrying, or accepting the risks involved in carrying it, risks that would affect not only her, but the rest of her family.

I thought she was a remarkable lady and suggested she make a decision within days rather than weeks. When Lillian and her husband were preparing to leave, she thanked me for all of the information and said she would make an appointment for the following Monday, four days away. I told her that would be all right.

The following Monday, Lillian came to my office, this time alone. She told me she had decided, with her husband's support, to continue the pregnancy. Her obstetrician had told her he would transfer her care to our office.

I asked her if she had any other questions, and she said all of her questions were answered. I told her we would gladly take care of her.

I spent some time with Lillian, instructing her as to what to look for and what signs or symptoms she should report to us without delay. We scheduled several ultrasound examinations to monitor the growth of the baby, and also the growth of the placenta, so that we could evaluate potential complications associated with placental growth. As Lillian did not work outside the home, I did not place any unusual restrictions on her activity.

We decided to follow her at regular, two-weekly intervals until later in pregnancy. Barring unforeseen circumstances, we planned for a delivery at or around thirty-six weeks of gestation.

Lillian became very popular in our office. No one on the staff had ever encountered a patient with an abdominal pregnancy, so they pampered her every time she was in the office; Lillian enjoyed the special attention.

The infant appeared to be doing well, although it was in the lower part of the expected growth curve, most likely because the placenta, while functional, probably had impaired function when compared with a normal placenta. However, as long as the baby' s growth was within normal limits, I was not planning to intervene. If the baby were to suddenly stop growing, it would force my hand to deliver the baby, since otherwise it could suffer from growth impairment. Lillian did not want to know the sex of her baby, so we kept that to ourselves. Nobody in the office knew it, apart from me. The ability to identify the sex of the unborn baby can be a plus for those parents who want to know. However, it would be a terrible disappointment if I revealed the sex of the baby to parents who did not wish to know and wanted to be surprised at birth.

Periodically, Lillian's husband would accompany her to her appointments. Each time, I was able to reassure him that Lillian was doing well and that the pregnancy was continuing within my expectations. He was a very caring individual. On one of theirs visits, they brought their two children with them and out office staff held a little party for them. Needless to say, the kids were impressed.

By the time Lillian reached thirty-three weeks, as expected she was beginning to be a little anxious. Without saying as much, it was obvious she was eager to be delivered as soon as it was safe to do so. Lillian and I discussed her earliest possible delivery date, and I told her that thirty-six to thirty-seven weeks would be safe for the baby. The neonatologists who would care for the newborn baby were comfortable with that plan. I told her I would see her twice a week, and that each time we would perform an ultrasound and other tests that would allow us to determine the baby's health.

Using ultrasound one can examine the cord blood flow to make sure it is normal. Also, I could look at the amount of amniotic fluid, and the baby's activity. Then we could proceed with what we call a Non-Stress Test, in which the activity of the baby is correlated with the fetal heartbeat reacting to the movements. If we have a normal heart, its heart rate will increase with the mother's exercise, and will return to normal when she rests. If that reaction is not present, we interpret it as the baby having some problems. Sometimes, intervention is necessary and delivery is initiated without delay.

Lillian's infant was doing well. Although its growth was slightly behind other babies at that age, it was still within acceptable limits.

At thirty-five weeks, we started making preparations for a delivery the following week. A cesarean section to deliver an abdominal pregnancy presents different challenges when compared to an intrauterine pregnancy. We had a pretty good idea of the extent of the placental implantation on Lillian's pelvic bone area, and the loop of bowels involved. We knew that the placenta had not reached the diaphragm—the muscle that separates the abdominal cavity from the chest.

We decided we would make no attempt to separate the placenta from the organs it had attached itself to, since that would create excessive bleeding, which we absolutely had to avoid. Once we delivered the infant, we would tie and cut the cord very close to where it attached to the placenta. and leave everything else as is. With the infant delivered, over time, the placenta would resorb itself and everything would return to normal. The resorption may take months or sometimes several years, so the risks of spontaneous bleeding remained, nonetheless. Since no one can anticipate bleeding, we had to be prepared for the worse and have the necessary blood available.

I spoke to the blood bank and told them what we were preparing for. They already had a sample of Lillian' s blood and assured me they would have enough blood available and ready for the day of the operation. Lillian wanted to know again how the surgery would be performed and whether she would require general anesthesia. Our anesthesiologists opted for having her asleep, and Lillian did not object. Her surgery was scheduled for the day that she reached thirty-six weeks.

Lillian was admitted to hospital the night before surgery. We made arrangements for her husband to spend the night in the hospital with her. At seven o'clock the next morning, everyone was in the operating room. I asked Lillian and her husband if they had any questions before we began. They did not, but they wished us all good luck.

I scrubbed and entered the operating room. When I got there, Lillian was already asleep. I proceeded to open her abdomen, and after inspecting the area around the amniotic sac—which is where the amniotic fluid and the infant are—to make sure there were no large vessels around, I opened the sac, drained the fluid, clamped the cord and removed the infant, a baby girl. Lillian had a healthy four pound, eleven ounces baby girl. The neonatologist was pleased.

After delivering the baby, I slowly followed the cord to the placenta and tied it as close to its insertion point with the placenta as possible. I then removed the excess cord.

I was happy to see that the operative field was dry. I waited for about ten minutes, inspecting the areas of implantation we had identified by prior ultrasound and checking for any others. There was no bleeding anywhere. Things were going our way!

I decided it was time to close Lillian's abdomen, which I did without any problems. Shortly after, Lillian was transferred to the intensive care unit for close monitoring, just in case the unthinkable happened. Fortunately, it did not. The next morning, I transferred her to the obstetrical floor.

Both Lillian and her husband were ecstatic. The baby girl was thriving and would be going home soon. Lillian was recovering quickly, and within days, I was planning to let her go home. Lillian's follow-up, however, would be a long-term one. Since her post-operatory course had been totally uneventful, I was optimistic the leftover placenta would not cause undue problems, but how long it would take to resorb, I could not predict. I was certainly delighted with the outcome. We were not completely out of the woods, since complications could still occur. In her case, fortunately, we did not have any serious problems. At six month checkup, Lillian told me that she and her husband decided that their family was complete. No future pregnancies for Lillian.

* * *

It's not my baby!

Once, three of our patients delivered on the same night and another had to be admitted because of some bleeding, I had to attend to two consultations from other doctors and a cesarean section on an emergency admission too, so given the workload, it was no surprise that I had been up all night. Usually, when on night call, I was able to catch some sleep, but this time, that had not been the case. The next morning, I was waiting for my partner to arrive to relieve me and looking forward to a few hours of good sleep when my beeper started buzzing without mercy. I looked at the screen to see who was paging me. It was our emergency room.

I picked up the phone and the clerk immediately transferred me to the emergency room physician.
"Dr. Aladjem, we need you here. Could you come, please?" he told me.
"What's the problem?"
He proceeded to tell me that, about twenty minutes ago, a woman had been admitted to the emergency room and complained of severe abdominal cramping that had started about three hours previously. He had seen her immediately, thinking he was dealing with what we call "an acute abdomen," like in a ruptured appendix or intestinal torsion. However, when he examined here, he discovered that she was pregnant and in labor.

"I told her she was pregnant and in labor, and she went ballistic, denying that she was pregnant or in labor," he continued. Apparently, she had created quite a disruption in the emergency room, yelling and screaming that she was dying and that nobody was helping her.
"I really need some help," he finally admitted. I told him I would be there in a few minutes.

Exhausted after a sleepless night, I was not looking forward to dealing with such a situation, but thought, *Well, that's the way things sometimes are.* I called the labor and delivery clerk and told her to tell my partner, when he arrived, to come to the emergency room, as that was where I was heading.

As I was turning the corner to the corridor that lead to the emergency room, I could hear a woman screaming. I thought to myself, *Dear God, I do hope that is not my patient.* In the waiting area, five patients were waiting to be seen. Looking at their faces, I figured they were probably thinking they should go somewhere else. I would not have blamed them; this was quite an unusual spectacle.

The receptionist told me that Dr. Wilson was in room two, with the patient I had been asked to see. I entered the room to find Dr. Wilson and two nurses trying to calm the patient down. She was struggling.

"I am dying! I am dying!" she was screaming. She looked at me. "Help me! Help me!" she yelled. Somehow she had decided that the people who had seen her so far were not helping her, and she did not trust them. She was desperately trying to get my attention.

I approached her immediately, took her hand, and told her, "Calm down, calm down. I am Dr. Aladjem." To everyone's amazement, she stopped struggling, resettled herself in bed and looked straight at me.

"Please, help me," she said.

"I will," I replied, reassuring her as much as I could. "What's your name?"

"Jenny. My stomach has been hurting since early this morning. Comes and goes. I hurt. What's wrong with me?" she pleaded.

"Let's find out," I told her. "Is anyone with you?"

The ER nurse helping Dr. Wilson, was about to answer. I signaled her with my hand to keep quiet. I needed the patient to tell me. "No one," she said. "I have no one."

It was apparent that she was starting to hurt again, so I put my hand on her abdomen. I could feel the uterus that was beginning to harden. I held her hand as tightly as I could and told her to breathe in and out until the pain was gone. She looked straight at me, with a fixed stare, and started breathing as instructed. She did that at an increasing rhythm as her uterus tightened more and more, and then slowed down as the contraction decreased in intensity.

"Tell me what happened," I asked. She proceeded to tell me that she had gone to bed at ten o'clock last night after having eaten a heavy meal of spaghetti and meatballs. She had cooked the meal fresh for herself, so it was not canned. "My food is always good," she told me. She was awoken by a bellyache at around three o'clock in the morning. She did not pay much attention, just thinking she had eaten too much spaghetti for dinner. She tried to fall asleep again, but could not, and decided that walking around the house might help speed her digestion; it did not help. The cramps were beginning to grow stronger and stronger, and by seven o'clock in the morning they had become very painful. Scared, she had decided to drive herself to the hospital.

"Here is another cramp coming," she said, almost in panic.

"Breathe again, as before," I instructed her. She did, and when I felt her uterus tighten, she let out a big scream and started breathing in and out very fast.

"Jenny," I told her, "we are going to look at your tummy with an ultrasound, and see what we can find out." I asked the nurse to bring the ultrasound machine.

During all this time, Dr. Wilson had not said a word. He moved backwards, toward the wall behind and instinctively knew that intervening might undermine the confidence Jenny was beginning to have in me. When the ultrasound was brought in, I asked Jenny to lie flat on her back. "Jenny, we are going to look at your tummy and see why you hurt," I informed her.

"What's that?" she asked. "It's a machine called an ultrasound, which will give us a picture of your tummy. It won't hurt at all," I reassured her.

"OK."

I turned the ultrasound on and scanned her abdomen. There it was: a baby that appeared full-term and looked to weigh seven or eight pounds. The head was down in the pelvis, and since I had not yet physically examined Jenny, I looked at the cervix too; it was almost completely dilated. We were close to delivery.

At that moment, my partner opened the door, looked at what was going on and asked me if I wanted him to take over.

"No, thank you. I think I'll finish this myself. I'll talk to you after that," I told him.

"Fine," he answered. "I'll be in labor and delivery."

I looked at Jenny. "Jenny do you want to take a look at what I can see?" I asked her.

"Sure," she answered.

"Stay the way you are," I told her. "I will move the screen so that you can see". I asked the nurse to push the machine towards the head of the bed, while I was keeping the picture on the screen. Turning the screen towards Jenny, I then pointed to the outline of the baby. "See, Jenny, you are going to have a baby. You have been pregnant and did not realize it. The pain you are having is because you are in labor."

For a moment, she looked at the screen and then she let go a terrible scream. "This is not my baby! I am not pregnant. You are a liar. Let me out of here, let me out of here."

It took Dr. Wilson, myself, and a nurse to hold her down; otherwise, she would have fallen off the bed onto the floor.

"You put the baby there! It's not my baby!" she continued to scream.

"Do you want me to sedate her a little?" Dr. Wilson said.

"Yes, please. Enough to sedate her, but not enough to put her to sleep."

Dr. Wilson gave an order to the nurse, who left and quickly returned with a syringe. Without delay, Dr. Wilson injected the sedative into Jenny's arm.

"We need an immediate psychiatric consult. Who is on call?" I asked. "Dr. Malvery," he said. I'll page him immediately."

By that time, Jenny had begun to feel the effect of the fast-acting sedative. I told the nurse we should prepare for a delivery right there. With her, and another nurse's, help, I gloved rapidly and was able to perform a quick vaginal examination. The baby's head was now in the pelvis.

213

"She will deliver shortly," I told them. "Let me have a gown and gloves. Call neonatology and tell them we have an emergency delivery here and that we need the neonatologist immediately. Also, call labor and delivery and ask them to send a nurse down here immediately with an emergency delivery pack."
The ER nurse who was helping me picked up the phone, called labor and delivery and relayed my instructions.

Jenny was half conscious and half asleep, but she was not screaming or fighting. The nurse from labor and delivery was there in no time, as were the neonatologist and neonatal nurse. "What's going on?" Dr. Naegle, the neonatologist, asked me. I summarized the situation as briefly as I could. "She'll deliver very soon," I added.

Everyone was ready for when the baby would be delivered and Dr. Wilson returned to tell me the psychiatrist was on his way.

I asked the labor and delivery nurse and the emergency room nurse to help by positioning Jenny so that I could deliver the infant. Each nurse held one of Jenny's legs to enable me to perform a vaginal exam. Dr. Wilson left the room and returned with another dose of sedative, just in case it was needed.

Jenny, still under the effect of the first sedative, was not fighting. I tried to see if she was coherent enough to understand what we are doing. "Jenny, we are going to deliver your baby. If you feel a tummy pain again, push as if you were to move your bowels," I told her. She must have heard something, but she just mumbled some unintelligible words. Yet somehow, more as a reflex from her contraction than a voluntary decision, she started pushing intermittently, each push accompanied by guttural sounds. "Mmhh. Mmhhhhh."

It was good enough. Nature takes over in cases like this. The head "crowned," came down onto the perineum, and the baby started it make its appearance. Our nurse had opened the emergency tray and asked me if I wanted the small forceps to help in the delivery. "I don't think we need it," I said. Sure enough, the head was almost out and a few minutes later I was able to deliver the infant without any effort.

I clamped and cut the cord, and handed the baby, a crying little girl, to the neonatologist. Jenny went straight to sleep and was still sound asleep when Dr. Malvery, the psychiatrist, arrived.
"It's been a while since I've seen a delivery. What's going on?" he asked.
I proceeded to give him a detailed history of what had happened. He listened carefully, asked a few questions, and said he would talk to Jenny once she recovered from her sedation. He then asked the neonatologist if it was a must for Jenny to breastfeed. Dr. Naegle responded that the baby did not necessarily need to be breastfed.
"Good, because Jenny will need some medications that cross into the breast milk and make breast feeing inadvisable."

I delivered the placenta and examined Jenny. She was all right. Dr. Malvery suggested that until he could assess her, we should not put her in with the baby. It sounded reasonable. Dr. Malvern's impression was that Jenny may have had a panic attack, or that she may have an underlying schizophrenia.
"Do you think we can take Jenny to the postpartum unit?" I asked.
"I think so. I will see her in about an hour on your unit." He added that he would write his orders once he'd had a chance to talk to her. I thanked him for coming. As a result of a combination of a sleepless night, exhaustion, and the sedation, Jenny was now sound asleep, which was good for her.

I thanked Dr. Wilson and his staff, asked Dr. Wilson to arrange Jenny's transfer to our unit, and left ER for labor and delivery, to talk to my partner.

"Quite a show," he said when he saw me.
"If you can call it that," I said. We talked for a while and I updated him on exactly what had happened with Jenny and what the psychiatrist had said, and I then asked him to take over. I also asked him to call social services to update them on what had happened. Their services were going to be crucial in what happened next and how Jenny and her infant were going to be managed.

215

I was tired. In fact, I was so tired that I did not feel it would be safe to drive home. I decided to call my wife and tell her I would have a few hours sleep at the hospital before returning home.

I woke up after about four hours and called my partner, who was in our office, to ask about Jenny. The psychiatrist had seen Jenny and his feelings were that she had suffered a panic attack. He did not think she was schizophrenic. She had apparently calmed down and was able to talk to the psychiatrist for about an hour. He ordered some tranquilizers, but did not think she would be prone to repeating the episode in the immediate future. He did suggest, however, that the prudent thing to do would be to bring the baby to her but keep a nurse there for the duration of the visit, which should be limited to fifteen minutes at most. The psychiatrist would see her again the next day, but he also wanted to talk to social services and see what temporary arrangements could be made for the baby, since he did not think Jenny was able to take care of the little girl for a while. That he did not think Jenny was schizophrenic, was good news.

I decided to go and visit Jenny before I went home. Her room was near the nurse's station, at the suggestion of the psychiatrist. I knocked on the door and entered. Jenny was awake and watching TV. "How are you, Jenny?" I asked.
"Good morning, doctor," she said. "I am really well."
Without being asked any questions, she spontaneously started talking. She apologized for the scene she had made in the ER, although much of it she did not remember. She told me she got pregnant after binge drinking, of which she had no recollection. When she missed her periods, she did not think about it. After a few months, she realized she might be pregnant, but convinced herself it was not possible. She never went to a clinic or a doctor, and she could not remember ever feeling the baby move. Yes, she thought she was gaining weight, but had attributed that to eating too much. When she started to not feel well the night before, she had panicked and came to the hospital hoping that she was sick. When someone told her that she was in labor, she really lost it. "I am so sorry," she said.

I told her that I trusted she would now recover under the care of the psychiatrist, and would not have anymore panic attacks. She told me that she had a job in a supermarket, and that she would be able to take care of her baby. "She will change my life," she said.

It was a sad story and incredible that her mind could place her in a state of total denial. I asked if she had any questions. "Not right now, thank you," Jenny answered.
"I will see you tomorrow, Jenny," I said. "Rest and recuperate."

The next morning, Jenny was seen by social services. They told me that, pending the psychiatrist's final evaluation, they would attempt to keep the baby in the nursery and would not start any placement procedure until the psychiatrist's evaluation was complete. They considered that was fair, and I agreed.

On the third day, I told Jenny that if the psychiatrist cleared the way, I could discharge her in a couple of days.
"I feel good," Jenny told me.
I knew the psychiatrist was seeing her on a regular basis, and I was looking forward to his evaluation. A couple of days later, he called me to let me know I could discharge Jenny. He felt Jenny did not have any mental illness and that her behavior in the ER was a panic attack resulting from her pregnancy denial. He did say, however, that the baby should remain in the nursery until his next evaluation in one week. Social services told him they would arrange that. There were no limitations to Jenny visiting the baby. I thanked him and asked him to send me a confirmatory note and he told me he would also make a note on the chart. The following day, I discharged Jenny and told her I would like to see her in six weeks for her postpartum check. Jenny was in high spirits, and thanked me for my help.
"Please give my apologies to the ER doctor."
I promised to do so.

Six weeks later, Jenny brought her baby in to the office with her. "Isn't she beautiful?" she said. I agreed. She was a lovely baby, neatly dressed and in good health. I knew that Jenny had been able to take her baby home a week after she herself had been

217

discharged. She continued to see the psychiatrist every month and would continue to do so for some time

"I really feel good," she told me. "They were very good at my job. They gave me a week off with full pay when I told them the baby was coming home."

Jenny was in good spirits, and I asked her if she wanted to use any contraceptives.

"Not right now. I broke up with my boyfriend. He was not good for me. Can I come back if I ever need any?" I reassured her that she could come back any time.

The next time I saw Jenny was a year later, when she came for a scheduled check. I would not have recognized her. She had lost weight, earned a promotion in her job, and the psychiatrist had discharged her completely. She brought her baby with her and it was indeed a nice reunion.

* * *

Who is the father?

It was the weekend before Thanksgiving, and it was my turn to be on call. Weekend calls can be unusual, in the sense that one is on call not only for our office but for any high-risk patient who may be arriving at the hospital without a designated physician. In addition, if a physician on the staff has a patient with a complicated pregnancy, we are usually called. We can, therefore, never predict what is going to happen and what patients we may have to care for. In a busy hospital like ours, the weekend before Thanksgiving is usually a challenging weekend.

I arrived at the hospital around eight o'clock in the morning and changed into my scrubs. Then I made my usual rounds, discharging patients who were supposed to go home that day, and taking care of those who had either delivered or had been hospitalized. There were no emergencies. I made my way to the labor and delivery area to check for messages or news about incoming patients. Things were quiet, and I was not complaining.

Having finished my rounds, I went to the doctor's lounge for a cup of coffee and some sweet rolls and sat there watching the morning news. Nothing very exciting.

It is an interesting psychological phenomenon, at least for me, that when things are quiet on call, I become restless. I was there to do something, yet I was doing nothing. It does not make sense, but that's the way it happens. Without anything to do, I went to the hospital records room. Surely, there must be some old charts I had to sign. The record room lady told me: "You have no open pending charts, Dr. Aladjem."
So much for that.

I finally decided to go to my office and do some reading. My desk always held the latest medical journals, which I had not yet found time to read, or some new textbook I had bought the month before. Noon came fast enough and—without fail—the labor and delivery clerk paged me while I was at lunch. A new patient was being admitted through the emergency room. She was in early labor, and she had no doctor.

"Can I finish my lunch?" I asked the clerk.

After a short pause, she came back. "The nurse says you can. No emergency, they'll start the routine."

"Thanks."

After lunch, I walked to labor and delivery. The only patient was the one just admitted. *Calm before the storm*, I thought to myself.

Melanie, the new patient, was a thirty-five-year-old woman who happened to be in town for the day when she had started contracting. She was a week away from her due date. Rather than going home, a little town some forty miles away, she thought she would check in the emergency room to our hospital. If she were not in labor, she would rather go home.

I asked the clerk to see if she could get a copy of Melanie's records from the hospital where she was supposed to deliver. A little while later, she came to tell me they would be faxing her records to us.

I did not feel it would be prudent to let Melanie drive herself home. The monitor showed regular contractions, which at that point, were mildly uncomfortable. She had no objection to staying with us and said she would call her boyfriend and her family to let them know where she was, and why.

This was Melanie's second pregnancy. Her first baby had been delivered by her family physician, three years beforehand. Melanie had not been aware of any problems during her first pregnancy, and this pregnancy had also been normal.

My examination showed she was in early labor that seemed to be progressing at a good pace. When I had first arrived in her room, her contractions had appeared to be only moderately uncomfortable, but they were now picking up in intensity and frequency. Melanie even had to stop talking when the contractions were reaching their peak—a sign of good labor, for sure. The infant was doing well, and the monitor showed that the baby's heart rate was normal with no apparent problems. Her cervix was already about four centimeters dilated, and the head was slowly descending into the pelvis.

I asked her whether she was a natural birth, or whether she would like to have an epidural. She said she had a natural childbirth with her first child and intended to do the same this time.

I told her that I would be in the hospital and would see her periodically or at any time she needed me. I reassured her that everything seemed to be fine and that I would expect her to deliver within three to four hours at most.

Before leaving the labor and delivery area, I told the nurse that Melanie wished to have a natural childbirth and asked her to give me an hourly report on Melanie's progress.

As I was leaving the unit, my cell phone rang. It was one of the staff physicians, who had a patient in the hospital and would appreciate a consult. I asked where she was and what her name was, and assured him I would see her without delay. I decided to go and see the patient while things were still relatively quiet.

Mrs. Simpson was her name, and she was on the antepartum unit, where undelivered patients are admitted. She was forty years old and in her first pregnancy. This is what we call "an elderly primigravida," which literally means "older woman in her first pregnancy." This is by no means a derogatory name. First pregnancies in a woman of that age have many potential problems. By giving them that name, we simply emphasize the potential problems such a patient might have.

Mrs. Simpson was now at term. She also had an underlying mild chronic hypertension—a problem common in an elderly primigravida. The question my colleague was asking was how long he could safely wait for labor to begin spontaneously without endangering the infant's well-being.

Unfortunately, such questions cannot be easily answered. Many factors have to considered before giving an opinion. In reviewing

Mrs. Simpson's chart, it appeared to me that certain tests to assess fetal well-being had not yet been performed. I ordered them to be carried out without delay. Then I called my colleague back and told him what I had ordered and why, asking him to call me as soon as the tests were completed. I told him that the issue was not so much whether she should be delivered, but how soon. He thanked me and said he would call me as soon as the tests were reported.

By the time I had finished seeing Mrs. Simpson, the labor and delivery nurse called me with her report of Melanie's progress. She was in good labor, and things were looking promising. Her admitting labs were normal and Melanie's boyfriend had arrived. She told me that there was also another gentleman in the room. "Nothing urgent, but you may want to come and meet them," she told me.
"Why?" I asked.
"Well, let me say it is an unusual situation, which you may want to be aware of," she said.
"Ok," I replied.

This was most unusual. I had no clue as to what was going on. Obviously, it had nothing to do with Melanie's labor, as Nancy just told me Melanie's labor was progressing well. *No point in speculating*, I thought, as I made my way to the room.

In the labor and delivery area, I looked at the clerk. She hardly noticed me and continued to do whatever she was doing. I went to Melanie's room. Upon entering, I introduced myself to the two men in the room. One of them shook my hand and said, "Nice to meet you. I am Denis, Melanie's boyfriend."
"Nice to meet you," I replied. Then I looked at the other fellow, who stood up and extended his hand. I shook his hand and said again, "I am Dr. Aladjem."
"Nice to meet you. I am Roger, Melanie's husband."
There was a long pause. I was not sure I understood, or how to react.
The man who said he was Melanie's husband, spoke first. "Let me explain, Doctor. Melanie and I separated about six months ago. Our

divorce has not yet been completed. For all we know, the baby may be mine and not Denis's."

I looked at Denis, who nodded. "As we stand now, I have to know if I have any obligations, moral or otherwise, to this new kid. That's why I am here. No hard feelings."

Wow! I had never been faced with such a situation in all my years of practice, not with any of the thousands of babies I had delivered. "How will being here will tell you whether the baby is yours or Denis's?" I heard myself saying. "I would like a DNA study carried out on the baby, on Denis and myself, as soon as the baby is born. Then we'll know."

I looked at Melanie. "Melanie, you heard our conversation, do you agree or have any objections?" As far as I was concerned, Melanie was my patient in this hospital, and I most certainly would not allow anything to be done without her approval.

Melanie immediately said, "That's fine with me. I don't know who the father is either."

"We all agree then," said Roger. "How do we do this?"

"I am sorry. You must understand that I have never been faced with such a situation. I am not a lawyer, so I'll have to consult with the hospital's lawyer. I will try to get hold of him and let you know," I replied, and then exited the room.

Nancy, the nurse assigned to Melanie followed me to the lounge. I looked at her and she looked at me.

"You should have seen your face when Roger introduced himself as Melanie's husband," she said.

"I need a cup of coffee," I responded.

"Let me make a fresh pot. It will only take a minute," Nancy said.

Word spread like fire among the staff and some of them walked into the lounge, smiling. The head nurse looked at me and, hardly able to hold back a laugh, said, "What kind of Peyton Place are you making out of labor and delivery?"

"Well, at least my calls are not boring," I responded. I finished my cup of coffee and stood up. "I have to call the hospital attorney," I said.

I returned to my office to call the attorney, Jim. I did not feel I could make this call from any other phone in the hospital. As it turned out, Jim was home. I told him what was going on and his first reaction was, "Oh my, that's a first for this hospital."

"That's a first for this doctor, too."

He asked if our labs could take a DNA specimen easily. I told him that should not be a problem. "Silvio, this is what we are going to do," he said and proceeded to tell me he would write a release of liability and permits to obtain DNA samples from all those involved, and would fax everything to the clerk in labor and delivery. All we would have to do is fill in the names. I would have to sign it, too, and the head nurse and another nurse chosen by the head nurse would sign as witnesses. A copy would go into the chart, and one to each of those who signed. The permit for the DNA taken from the baby would have to be signed by the mother only, since it was not clear whom the father was.

"It will take me an hour or so before I can fax it," Jim said.

"Thanks, Jim. Have a nice weekend."

"You too," he answered.

To relax for a few minutes, I turned the radio to my favorite station. It was broadcasting from the Metropolitan Opera—the *Barber of Seville*. I love this opera, so I stood there for about half an hour listening to the bubbling music, full of life, zest, and effervescence and thought that Rossini would have written a wonderful comic opera out of Melanie's story. Then, knowing I had to go back, I turned the radio off and headed for labor and delivery. When I got there, the clerk told me that Nancy believed Melanie would be ready to deliver very shortly. I told the clerk let me know as soon as she received a fax from the hospital attorney. She acknowledged my instructions.

In Melanie's room, Nancy was coaching Melanie with her breathing and pushing. Nancy told me Melanie was close to delivery and that the membranes were still intact. Baby was doing well.

I turned to Denis and Roger and explained what we were going to do. Then I asked Melanie if she wanted either of the two fellows in the room during delivery. Melanie said they should do whatever they preferred. Both Denis and Roger decided to sit in the waiting area, and left the room.

I put a glove on and examined Melanie. She was completely dilated and the baby's head was on the perineum. I signaled to Nancy that I was going to break the membranes. In no time, the labor room was transformed into a delivery room. Two more nurses came in for extra help if needed and the clerk alerted the neonatology service of an impending delivery.

Melanie continued to push with each contraction, relaxing in between contractions, and reserving her strength to push at their peak, which is the most efficient push a laboring mother can do. With each contraction, the baby's head was descending a little more each time. Her perineum began to stretch, and I knew it was a matter of a few more contractions before she would deliver. Nancy's coaching was superb, as usual, and we were making exceptionally good progress in a short time. I examined Melanie again, and by now thought that she should give birth with the next contraction. I asked Melanie to hold her breath with the peak of her next contraction and then push long and sustained. She did so, and sure enough, the little head made its appearance and was easily delivered. It was a little boy, whom I handed to the neonatology nurse after cutting the cord.

The infant's cry filled the room and Melanie was relieved. After the baby was cleaned, he was put into Melanie's arms. The placenta delivered soon after, and it was apparent that there were no tears or any problems.

I congratulated Melanie, who thanked me apologized for all that had happened. She had not expected her husband to come. No harm done. I repeated the plans for receiving the documents from the hospital lawyer. She had no problem with any of the proceedings we had to undergo.

I made my way to the waiting area, and for the first time in my life, had to congratulate two potential fathers without knowing who the infant's real father was.

About two hours later, the documents Jim had prepared arrived by fax. I looked at them, and asked the head nurse whom she would choose for the other nurse witness. She told me that Nancy, who had taken care of Melanie's delivery, would be a good choice, and Nancy had no objections. The three of us went to Melanie's room. She was comfortable and accompanied by the two gentlemen.

I handed to each of them the document they would have to sign. Both men and Melanie read it, and signed it without any objection. Nancy, the head nurse and I signed them as witnesses and then I handed each of them their copy and placed one in the chart. When we were all done, I called the lab and told them what we needed to do. They were there in no time and took a buccal smear from the two gentlemen and from the infant.

Melanie had an uneventful postpartum course. The baby, weighing seven pound, six ounces, went home with the mother, still not knowing its father. Melanie asked if it would be OK for her to see her own doctor for her six weeks postpartum check, and I said that would be acceptable.

We never did learn who the father was.

* * *

What's for dinner?

One day I was on call after a good friend, Dr. Mark, called me early in the morning and asked if could cover his practice for the day. He had to leave town unexpectedly and would not return until the following morning. He had no patients in the hospital and the first due date of a patient was ten days away. That patient was Mrs. Pentworth, whose pregnancy had progressed without incident, and whose records were already available in the labor and delivery record room.
I said that I would be happy to do so, and asked him to call me on his return so that I could provide an update, should anything happen.

Just in case, I went to the record room and looked for Mrs. Pentworth's chart. She was in her thirties and was thirty-eight weeks pregnant with a perfectly normal pregnancy, her third. I made a point to let the clerk know I would be covering for Dr. Mark for the day and then made my rounds and put Mrs. Pentworth's pregnancy in the back of my mind. I did not expect to see her that day.

By early afternoon, a call from labor and delivery alerted me that Dr. Mark's patient, Mrs. Pentworth, was there and was feeling contractions. I thought it was probably false labor (when contractions are present but not intense enough to qualify as labor contractions and usually subside); in such cases, observation is all that is needed before discharging the patient. False labor seemed to fit Mrs. Pentworth's story.

I went upstairs to labor and delivery and introduced myself, informing her that Dr. Mark was out of town, and that, if she did not mind, I would be taking care of her. She had no objection to me taking care of her. To my surprise, she was in early labor rather than in false labor. Her contractions were frequent enough and strong enough but had not yet produced any changes in the cervix. The infant seemed fine. I asked if her husband would be there during her labor, and she acknowledge that indeed he would. He had just gone out to complete an errand and she expected him back at any moment.

I shared my impression that she was in very early labor, and that if it continued she would go into full-blown labor in a matter of hours. I also inquired whether she wanted any pain medication or whether she desired a natural childbirth. She told me that both of her children were born naturally, and she would be fine having natural childbirth with her current pregnancy as well. I wrote a few standard orders and told the nurse I would be in the hospital should she need me, otherwise, I would return in two hours.

It was close to noon and I was hungry, so I went to the cafeteria for an early lunch and then decided to take a nap. Before I knew it, I was sound asleep. I must have slept for a couple of hours before I was awoken by the telephone.
The nurse in charge of Mrs. Pentworth was on the line. "Dr. Aladjem, I need you here. We have a situation."
"What's wrong."
"You have to come, and see for yourself."
That exchange was indeed odd. Mrs. Pentworth was by now in good labor and there was nothing wrong with her, according to the nurse, so what on earth could it be?

I washed my face and strode to the labor and delivery area. Nancy, Mrs. Pentworth's nurse, was waiting for me at the desk.
"What's going on?"
"Well, it's most unusual," she said. "Mr. Pentworth is in the room and he has brought with him a small electric stove and a frying pan!" She paused, waiting to see what affect her words were having on me.
"An electric stove and frying pan? What on earth are you talking about?"
"Well, Mr. and Mrs. Pentworth believe that everything has to be natural," she told me. "After delivery, he wants to cook the placenta so Mrs. Pentworth can eat it." Again she paused to see what I had to say. "

That's a new one," I said in disbelief. "They can do whatever they want with it after I have examined it, but I do not believe we can let them cook it in the room. The Fire Marshall will not approve."
"Let's go and talk to them," I told Nancy.

Nancy followed me into the room. I greeted Mr. Pentworth. "As your wife probably told you, Dr. Mark is out of town for the day, so I will take care of your wife."
"Yes, she did," he said.
"The nurse told me you and your wife believe in eating the placenta after the birth of the child. Is that correct?" I asked.
"Yes. She wants to do that. As you know, doc, the placenta is a very important organ and is full of good things for the woman who just gave birth."
"Well, if you believe it's that good, there is no point frying it. All the good things, hormones and the like, will be destroyed by the heat of cooking," I said.
That took him by surprise. "What do you mean?" he asked.
I proceeded to tell him that animals (although not all of them) eat their placenta for various reasons. First, they do not want to leave a trace of a new baby that might attract predators. They also eat their placenta because it is full of hormones and some vitamins, which helps the animal recover faster and allows for faster milk production and other things related to the immediate period after delivery. Animals, of course, do not cook, so they are eating the raw placenta and obtain the full benefits. People who advocate eating the placenta, because it is naturally good for the mother, forget that once you cook it, all those good hormones and vitamins are literally "cooked" out, and have no value. "Besides, Mr. Pentworth, the Fire Marshall will not look favorably on you cooking in a hospital room. We have smoke detectors all over the hospital. Your cooking could very easily be picked up by those sensors, and then we'd have the Fire Department trucks here in the parking lot in no time, which would not be funny. I cannot let you do that."

There was a long silence before he reacted as I hoped he would. "Well, I guess I won't do it here," he said.

Mrs. Pentworth was in labor and I do not think she really cared one way or the other. She did not say one word during my conversation with her husband.

"I'll be around when I am needed," I told them, and left the room, followed by Nancy.

"Is everything you told him true?" Nancy asked.

"Most of it," I replied, smiling. "Certainly the Fire Marshall part makes sense to me." I continued to tell her that eating the placenta—or placentophagia—is rare for humans. Most scientists will tell you that it is of no nutritional value, some naturalists have a different idea. In fact, Chinese medicine has used dried placental medicine for thousands of years for infertility and other disorders. In western civilization, claims have been made that it prevents postpartum depression, slows postpartum bleeding, and a host of other benefits. In the US, eating the placenta was a fad for a while on the west coast. In practice, however, its use is negligible. No scientific studies have been ever produced to substantiate—or negate, for that matter—the value of postpartum placentophagia. Its promoters have no more supportive documentation than its detractors.

"You live long enough," Nancy said "and eventually you see everything."

Mrs. Pentworth continued to labor and delivered late in the afternoon—a healthy seven pound baby boy.

"Would you like for me to save your placenta?" I asked her.

"No, thank you" she answered.

* * *

Special staff for a special task

Labor and delivery is an area where healthcare professionals work together twenty-four hours a day, sometimes under unbelievable stress and pressure. Working in such an environment, it is not surprising that labor and delivery staff are very special people, with special bonds.

One could make the case that labor and delivery areas are the same as any other departments of a hospital: there are clerks, nurses, physicians, and, of course, patients. However, a labor and delivery area is like no other. The vast majority of patients are healthy, waiting for that magical moment when they become a mother. This is where babies make their arrival into the world, signaling their arrival with their first cry. Lives change, women become mothers and men become fathers, something neither were trained for. Definitely, labor and delivery is an area more joyous than any in the hospital.

This peculiar environment affects all of us who are privileged enough to work there. Clerks are jovial well-wishers for incoming patients and get to know each patient. Nurses establish a special bond with mothers- and fathers-to-be, and those who are mothers themselves, reassure patients who are experiencing birth for the first time. If a patient has given birth there before, she probably remembers the names of the nurses who cared for her the last time, and most likely will ask if "Mary" or "Nancy" is still working there.

Physicians have already established a bond with their patients over the preceding nine months and get to know the family. Pregnant women can become very upset if their doctor is not there and they have not been informed in advance. Even in a practice with several obstetricians, patients tend to bond with one individual and will request a particular obstetrician attends at delivery. We respect that request whenever possible. Even if an obstetrician is not on call for labor and delivery on the day the patient goes into labor, we make every effort to honor their request. Whatever we can do, as physicians, to put the expectant mother at ease, we will do.

SILVIO ALADJEM MD

Sometimes problems arise. A mother may become very sick, or a baby may be unwell. Such incidents become immediately known throughout the entire staff, and as such, it becomes everybody's problem.

"How's the lady in room six?" or "Did someone tell the father?" or "Doc, do you think she'll make it?" Concern seems to grip every member of the staff. Aloofness is not a word known to a labor and delivery area.

But there is more to what makes a labor and delivery area such a special place. At all times there is a spirit of "we are all in this together"—nurses, doctors, and clerks. It is an interesting phenomenon that even technicians and ancillary service people, who have been assigned to labor and delivery and come there repeatedly during a twenty-four-hour period, absorb this spirit for the time they are there. Days later, after their tour of duty in labor and delivery is complete, it is not unusual for one of them to ask, "What did Mrs. Jones have, boy or girl?"

The birth of a child is something special for everyone—always.

It is natural that, in such an environment, interpersonal relationships create an unspoken bond, a bond we all recognize but take for granted in some ways and find difficult to define. Physicians are eager and available to help each other, no questions asked. Nurses go out of their way to make the doctor's job easier in some way or another.

It is not unusual to find that someone has brought in two dozen donuts for everyone to share in the coffee room, or maybe a basket of fruit, a box of candy, or even just a twelve-pack of diet coke. People on night shift often bring food—enough to feed a dozen people, not just themselves—to make sure that those who get busy and hardly have time to breathe, can relax in the lounge for a moment and eat something in between contractions. Often I arrived in the middle of the night to see a patient, only to have the clerk greet me with, "There's some food in the lounge, doctor, if you are hungry. It's good. Mary brought it."

Whether you had dinner before you came in is not important. When you work nights, you are always hungry.

Holidays are always special, too. Even though people are working over the holidays, there is always a party atmosphere and the two or three people who have had the luxury of a break make a point to greet the others, ask about their families, and show on-call staff pictures of their own kids opening presents, as well as wishing them a Happy Holiday. The lounge, without fail, has been decorated by someone from earlier shift.

Sometimes, not all is well in the world. Ginger's kid is sick. Joan had an accident and is in intensive care. Gail's father passed away. When this happens, it affects everyone in labor and delivery. You feel it. It's your family away from home. For days, it will be the topic of conversation.
"Did you go to see Joan? How is she?"
"Gail's father was a very nice man. He had a good life."
"How's Ginger's daughter doing?"
"Is there anything I can do?"

On occasion, this special bond between the labor and delivery area staff becomes personal. I remember my 60th birthday. I was making rounds on the obstetrical floor, when a page came that I was needed in labor and delivery immediately. I was on the second floor. All elevators were busy. Not knowing why I was needed I decided to run up the two floors. As I entered labor and delivery, the clerk immediately told me: "You are wanted in room 3" Without any hesitation I went to room 3 and opened the door and….a chorus of "Happy Birthday Dr. Aladjem" filled the room. The entire staff was there cheering and laughing. The cake was delicious. The memories, priceless.

As time goes by, people retire or change jobs, and others take their place. It takes a few days to learn the names of the newcomers, but they are always welcome to the group and soon fit in seamlessly. There is no special training; one just fits in by example. A week later, it will seem as if the newcomer has been there forever.

Yes, the labor and delivery area is special, and the staff members are special too. Such a team supports a doctor's efforts unconditionally, cheers when a new baby is born, is efficient as a well-oiled machine when the chips are down and time is of the essence, and breathes a sigh of relief when everything turns out well. And should a battle be lost, such a team grieves personally.

I feel very privileged to have known such extraordinary people over my career, and having spent forty years of my life in labor and delivery, despite my bias, I can say there is no other hospital area like a labor and delivery area.

* * *

AUTHOR'S NOTE

In the introduction to this book, I shared the essence of my feelings about how obstetrics, and helping bring so many new lives into the world, affected my life as an individual and as a professional. Having reached the end of the book, I pause to reflect on what I have written. Will these stories touch you? Will you be able to feel compassion for some, happiness for others? I do hope that, somehow, you will.

I look to these stories not only as my own personal memories, but as something worth telling, whether they occurred last year or thirty years ago. The passage of time is an interesting phenomenon; we all look at it from different angles, and it affects us all in different ways. I can look at the future and see the past. You may look at the past and see the future. Who is right? We both are!

Every birth encapsulates the past while looking into the future. Babies grow up and become parents, mothers get older and become grandmothers. The circle of life continues, and it all starts in the delivery room with the birth of a child.

Maternity, or maternal instinct, is something women are capable of long before they become pregnant. But it is only when they become pregnant that the true meaning of motherhood fills their body and spirit. Fatherhood is different: not any less important, but life-changing in a different way. A patient of mine once remarked when referring to her husband: "We are both looking forward to the birth of our baby, but it is different for him. Only I felt the baby's first movement inside me; I am a mother."

Every woman expects her pregnancy to be normal; after all, babies have been born since the dawn of time. Problems during pregnancy do occur, however, and most new mothers rarely think about that. "I'll be fine. You worry too much," is the standard motto of most pregnant women. Society itself is even good at ignoring the fact that complications in pregnancy do occur. There are books about pregnancy, more than any woman really needs, but the vast majority of them either do not mention potential problems, or perfunctorily refer to some, such as miscarriages, preeclampsia and a few other common problems, while ignoring the rest. Few could be considered to offer full disclosure.

When a pregnancy does not follow a normal course, it is common for people to think that somebody must be at fault. Since women, not men, have the babies, it follows that it must be the woman's fault. Some women are, therefore, brainwashed into feeling guilty if their pregnancy falls outside what is "normal." In truth, there is rarely any guilty party. Our society must start speaking openly about the fact that, sometimes, pregnancy is not normal. Mothers need support, not guilt.

Over the past twenty to thirty years, there has been a push for minimal intervention in pregnancy—as if delivering in a hospital, monitoring, and other technologies, create the complications. This is both foolish and dangerous. The sole purpose of obstetrical care is to have a healthy mother and a healthy baby. If anything, medical advances have reduced maternal and fetal mortality, and have improved general care for the mother, the fetus, and the newborn. As a result, more pregnancies are "normal."

Some of the stories included show how mothers cope with such difficulties. I do believe that mothers, who have had the misfortune to carry a pregnancy fraught with issues, become special mothers; they do not take their kids for granted. They will go that extra mile to make them happy and protect them. They will forever be thankful for the gift of providence.

And so, we come to the end of the road. I have enjoyed it immensely, and I hope you did too.

* * *

ACKNOWLEDGEMENTS

To my wife, Judith, for conceiving the idea of the book, and for her faith that I can do it.

To my editor Ms. Karin Cox, for her thoroughness, attention to details, suggestions and for making the manuscript what it is.

To my many friends, who along the way encouraged me and served sometime as sounding board as the book progressed, thank you.

Last, but not least, to the Staff of Author House, too many to mention individually. Thanks for your patience, care in production, and for making it become a reality.